Werner Kolb

Hey there! It's me, Musician with Tinnitus

AF239153

Werner Kolb

Hey there! It's me, Musician with Tinnitus

What it took from me and what it gave –
a travelogue

Bibliographic information of the German National Library:
The German National Library lists this publication in the German
National Bibliography; detailed bibliographic data is available on
the Internet at dnb.dnb.de.

Typesetting:	Werner Kolb
Cover Design:	Werner Kolb
Front Cover Photo:	Paintpictures / Pedi Wlosik
Back Cover Photo:	Mark Wohlfahrt Hanf, 2019

Publisher: BoD • Books on Demand GmbH, In de Tarpen 42, 22848 Norderstedt
Printed by: Libri Plureos GmbH, Friedensallee 273, 22763 Hamburg

ISBN: 978-3-7597-8463-6

www.werner-kolb.de
www.youtube.com / @wernerkolb

Table of Contents

Information is not knowledge
Knowledge is not wisdom
Wisdom is not truth
Truth is not beauty
Beauty is not love
Love is not music
Music is
THE BEST

—

<small>FRANK ZAPPA</small>
Packard Goose
›Joe's Garage Act III‹

Prologue

»The best thing to do is to put on headphones and turn the music up so loud that you can no longer hear your tinnitus. Otherwise, your brain will quickly memorize the sounds and burn them into your cerebral cortex. Then you can't do anything about it. Then it becomes chronic.«

That was the first piece of medical advice I received on the phone. Crazy, but true. In the list of statements from trained professionals, it stands unchallenged at the top. In comparison, slogans such as ›You'll have to live with it now‹ seem almost banal.

It was the first time in my life that I had to deal with this destructive way of communication. Both in medical and bureaucratic terms. And I have to admit that I had my problems with it.

I was born on March 23, 1963 in Aalen, Baden-Württemberg, at ten o'clock in the evening. In 1965, my family moved to neighbouring Ellwangen.

I have never been seriously ill so far. Apart from the usual childhood illnesses, I often suffered from middle ear infections as a teenager. There are voices claiming that this could be an indication that stress was already affecting my ears back then.

One night at the age of nineteen, I got extreme pain in my right foot. To this day, the worst I've ever experienced. The joint in my big toe was the source.

»Your purine levels are not elevated in any way, but the symptoms are clear – gout.«

I came into contact with alcohol and dope at an early age. It felt like excessive drinking and smoking weed was prevalent in my hometown across all social classes. But maybe I just never met the others.

My elevated liver fat values, which were sometimes very pronounced, always caused doctors to frown.

In March 2003, after one of my countless binges and a subsequent gout attack, they reached an all-time high.

»Mr. Kolb, you must immediately go to the ›Bernhard-Nocht-Institut‹ for observation.«

Instead, I decided to take a break from alcohol, which has lasted to this day.

»When was the last time you drank alcohol?«

Dr. Hans Pielke, my GP, looked at me through his slightly oversized glasses.

»Thirteen years ago.«

Every time he asked this question, another one was added. He looked at the results of the last lab test with a serious expression.

»Well, let's go ahead and do a biopsy then.«

On this occasion, I had to stay in the hospital overnight for the first time in August 2016.

»The bad news: we haven't found anything.
The good news: we haven't found anything.«

I was a chain-smoker for ten years, ›Schwarze Hand‹. One night, when I was twenty-three years old, I had a coughing fit that lasted about thirty minutes and was accompanied by severe shortness of breath. I had experienced something similar before. This time, however, it was so severe that the next morning I threw the remaining tobacco in the rubbish. I said to myself that nicotine was okay when smoking weed, and it actually worked. I never smoked a normal cigarette again.

In turn, I stopped smoking weed in 2013. After thirty-five years, I had to admit that I had been feeling more and more depressed whenever I consumed.

Since then, I have been what is colloquially referred to as ›clean‹. This may sound too simple for some. But I just didn't feel like it anymore. It's crazy how easy things can be when there is willpower.

The Holiday

September 9, 2016. The call resounded through the idyllic evening. A beautiful, atmospheric sound. With absolute silence in my head, I sat on a bench in front of my hut and took in the atmosphere of the Innsbruck Alps.

The sun was about to set and fog was beginning to cover the pastures when the young shepherd appeared next to me. He must have been in his early twenties and was wearing one of those classic ›Seppl-Hats‹. Hard to believe, I enjoyed it when he sang his melody and clapped his hands rhythmically. There was no distorted shrieking coming through to me, no pain in my ear canals.

As if out of nowhere, the first cows appeared from behind a hill and looked in our direction. One by one, they followed their shepherd's call to disappear into the barn with him before returning to their pastures the next morning. Fascinating.

For years, I had felt the desire to escape the constant noise and pressure of the big city, to find peace and quiet, to have time for myself, and to be creative. I was familiar with the Alps from my childhood, as my parents used to take me on ski holidays to Switzerland regularly

In autumn 2015, I spent a few days in the Allgäu and visited Daniel, whom I had reconnected with via social networks after more than thirty years. As we sat in his reading room and talked about the past, I decided to spend my time-out in the mountains. Together with Petra, my girlfriend, I tracked down this collection of small huts.

There aren't many events that gave me a queasy feeling – you could also call it fear. When I went hang gliding in a

Tunisian hotel complex many years ago, it took hours until I could breathe normally again. It was the only package holiday I had ever booked in my life. Due to my life philosophy based on freedom of choice, I actually reject this kind of holiday planning.

The last stage of my journey to the Grafensalm, which had nothing to do with a package holiday, was another example of this. I left the main road and began the ascent. The road I was travelling on became narrower and narrower and the verges increasingly brittle. There were no longer any crash barriers. Finally, I found myself on a gravel track. It wound round the mountain in serpentines and dropped off sharply down the sides.

»Two lorries can drive past each other«, laughed the dairyman when I told him about it during a neighbourhood chat. An elderly man who was making his retirement life more enjoyable. My blood would start to boil even if I had to manoeuvre past an oncoming Fiat Uno.

I was in this isolated place for a week, of course far too short. The tinkling of the bells that every cow wore around its neck and the sound of the mountain streams were the predominant sources of noise. The further I moved away from the huts and into the mountains, the quieter it became.

At night, when the sky was clear, I would sit outside my hut. I remembered as a little boy looking out of the window in the back seat of my parents' car and watching the stars. That's how I used to switch off so that I didn't have to listen to all the nagging from the front seats.

Even now, the world up there captivated me and I began to dream. That it would be pretty much the last time to be able to enjoy such peace and quiet was not mentioned.

***

›Are you the BEATLES- or the ROLLING-STONES-type?‹ When it comes to this frequently asked question, I clearly belong to the first category.

From the age of eight, I got classical piano lessons, which only fascinated me to a limited extent. Then I saw the film ›A Hard Day's Night‹ and I'm sure that this event triggered my love of music. According to Wikipedia, its first broadcast on German television was on Thursday, April 18, 1974. That makes sense, as I was eleven years old at the time.

Just one year later, hard rock was my island of security. I discovered the fascination of the local record store and my vinyl collection began to grow. My room was located in the basement under the garage, the place where I was undisturbed. When I came home from school, the first thing I did was put a record on the turntable, then lay down on my mattress: ›Deep Purple in Rock‹, *Speed King*, the intro – I closed my eyes, began to forget everything around me and immersed myself in the music. For twenty minutes, I was in a world that allowed my imagination to flow. It was only the sound of the tone arm announcing the end of the record side that brought me back. My mother signed me out of piano lessons, which was a sensible decision.

I had my first blackout experience with Daniel. To be more precise, on July 23, 1977, on the eve of the ›1st Rock-palast Night‹. We were fourteen and my parents were away for the weekend.

There was this house bar in our living room. It had the shape and appearance of a globe, the two halves of which soon no longer fitted together due to the frequent opening. We were intrigued by the rum with eighty percent of alcohol content.

»Hey, let's have a sip.« It tasted awful, but manly. One schnapps followed another.

»Down in one!«

I didn't see the concert itself. At the time, I was lying between my vomit and overturned flower pots.

Since then, I've had an ambivalent relationship with RORY GALLAGHER.

For my fifteenth birthday, my grandfather gave me a ›Viscount Intercontinental‹ organ. I was soon playing it in a band. That was one of the reasons why Daniel and I lost sight of each other. However, the contact was more sporadic anyway. Unlike me, he never touched alcohol again after our rum interlude. The other members of the band were about five years older than me and belonged to the post-hippie-generation; few parents wanted their children to socialize like that.

»Do you want some?«

I was on my way to Stuttgart with Jack and Uli. Uli turned to me from the passenger seat of the old Daimler with the gear stick on the steering column and held out his home-made hash pipe. I've already smoked joints at parties before, but had never felt anything. This time, however, it burned like hell when I inhaled.

»You have to take a big drag until the piece is completely burnt up,« Uli said with a grin, as if he knew what was going to happen to me and that it would be the first time. Jack pulled into a car park.

»Give me some too.« There was no mistaking that he was very experienced at this. He put in a cassette: FRANK ZAPPA's ›One Size Fits All‹. To the sound of *Inca Roads*, I sank into the cushions of the back seat and only regained my wits when we reached our destination a good hour later.

When I was seventeen, I went to Lake Como with several mates during the summer holidays. Roland, whose shoulder-length blond hair looked amazingly well-groomed, had LSD trips in his luggage. After a few fun and carefree days, we sat around having a cosy hangover breakfast.

»Do you fancy a trip?« What a stupid question.

»Dude, how long does it take for the effects to kick in? We swallowed the pill an hour ago and I don't feel anything yet.«

I walked over in a daze. What a world, lasting until the next morning. It was the ultimate enhancement of everything I had experienced so far. I loved it, this world. At least for four years. But then the trips started to become more and more unpleasant, and I decided to leave this drug in the past.

After leaving school, I did my community service. I underwent an examination of conscience in front of a five-member panel. Apparently, I answered the most absurd questions sufficiently to be accepted at the first hearing of this Punch and Judy show. So the consultation at the Ellwangen Youth Centre had served its purpose.

Just one day after receiving the registration for military service, I dropped my application for conscientious objection in the letterbox. I had already made the decision long beforehand. The same applied to my professional future. I wanted to leave the Swabian province and become a musician as soon as possible.

***

»Do you think I can have the room?«

It was January 14, 1985, and I was visiting Ebbe, an old football club mate who had been studying in Hamburg for a few months. His room consisted of a desk and a shelf crammed with books and records, but there was no record player. The inventory was rounded off by his futon mattress, which was rolled up in the corner during the day. My sleeping bag also found its place here.

He lived in a building with several separately rented furnished rooms, with the tenants sharing the kitchen and bathroom. I hadn't planned that. While we were chatting, it turned out that one of the rooms was empty.

»Why don't you ask?«

Two days later, he delivered the message that changed everything: »I've spoken to the landlord, it's fine.«

This was followed by one of my five-minute decisions, the consequences of which I couldn't even begin to comprehend.

I travelled back to southern Germany, gave notice on my room in a shared flat, which I had been living in for almost two years, and packed. My parents weren't as enthusiastic, but they didn't try to stop me either.

On January 28, 1985, I drove in my R6 to my new life. I was twenty-one and had never been to a metropolis like this before, apart from a few parties organized by friends who had mostly moved to bigger cities because of their studies.

I enrolled for ›Afrikanistik‹. It was the only degree program I found that did not have a ›Numerus clausus‹. I would often go to the main university building in the morning. There was a large notice board with job offers posted on it. Some of them were for the day in question, others for a longer period. I read through them and tore one off. I would then call the number from the nearest phone booth and head to work.

The jobs were usually for construction work. Of course, this was not at all conducive to keeping my hands supple, but no matter. I toiled the day away and received my wages in cash. I typically went to the supermarket to stock up the fridge.

One of my first jobs was restoring war graves from the First World War. Even when I was at school, I worked in gardening and landscaping during the summer holidays. I bought my first bass with the money I made back then. I have no idea why. I just felt like it. And it immediately became my instrument, it had far more sex than the black and white keys.

My engagement lasted one week, and every morning I travelled to Ohlsdorf cemetery. When cleaning the gravestones, I noticed the often young age of those buried here. Some were just fifteen years old. An age that was not so long ago for me and was characterized by parties and carefree living.

After that week, I was offered the chance to stay with the company for longer, but I didn't accept. I only wanted to work occasionally. I wanted to focus exclusively on my music. It wasn't difficult to get jobs at that time.

***

Ultimately, I don't do anything different today, only the nature of the jobs has changed over time.

In November 2016, I travelled across the Atlantic on a cruise ship for twelve days and then played gigs into December. For this, I used customized ear protection for my ear canals, which I had made three years earlier. By changing the filters, I could vary the attenuation between six dB and twenty-five dB, but it obviously didn't help or prevent anything.

A process must have started in me at some point, gradually. I can't say how long it had been going on. But I do know when I first noticed it.

The Suspicion

As all the live playing became more and more exhausting, I decided to build up an additional financial pillar. In 2015, I finished my training as a sound engineer and invested a five-figure sum to set up an acoustically optimized room in my 65 m² flat. Here I worked on productions, did exercises to train my ears or simply listened to music. The latter almost like before. The only difference was that I was no longer lying on a mattress, but sitting in an office chair.

On December 15, 2016, at the age of fifty-three years, eight months and twenty-two days, my life changed, even though I didn't realize it at the time. I made myself comfortable, started a sound experience from the forge of Bruce Swedien, Michael Jackson's sound engineer, and closed my eyes. However, what came out of the speakers was anything but a feast for the ears. It sounded as if my monitoring system, which was only three months old and cost more than three thousand euros, had malfunctioned. The voices sounded overdriven, surprisingly not all the music. After a few minutes, I ended the session and moved on to other things.

The next day, I sat down again – shit! Annoyed, I got my old speakers and amplifier out of the cellar to try and find the cause of the problem. Despite replacing the individual components and conducting a series of tests, I was unable to achieve a satisfactory result. In every configuration, the voices sounded as if they were being played through a megaphone that had been dropped multiple times. I did not consider looking for the issue within myself.

Days later, having postponed troubleshooting indefinitely, I listened to music with the headphones on – also distorted. It seemed unlikely to me that both the headphones and speakers were defective at the same time. The suspicion towards my ears began to grow.

***

When I came to Hamburg in 1985, there was a live club on Karolinenstraße called ›Let's Rock‹. Ebbe was a regular.

»Do you want to come with me?«

»Is there anything to smoke?«

»For sure. Herbert always comes by as a part of his evening round.«

That sounded like a land of milk and honey.

We went downstairs to the catacombs. Steve, the landlord, was waiting for us on the other side of the front door. He was chubby, had a moustache, and a thinning hairline. I guessed he was in his late twenties.

The ›Let's Rock‹ was a dive bar with no natural light, which was certainly a good thing. I didn't see a stage, just a drum kit in an otherwise empty room to the left of the bar. When there were no concerts, people jammed here. There was no pay, but the beer was free.

We went inside the sparsely filled dining room and sat down. I looked curiously at the posters on the lime-plastered walls. With a broad grin, Steve brought the beers.

»Are you the bass player Ebbe told me about? Jimmy's coming today, he's already looking forward to play with you.«

Monty, a well-known drummer on the scene, was sitting at one of the other tables with two broads. He never went home without finishing a bottle of tequila.

Then came Jimmy – singer, guitarist, bon vivant, and chatterbox. He was able to meticulously explain how the show business works.

»What do you say we go for a little spin?«

»What do you want to play?«

»*Red House*, everything else will fall into place. But you can only play the song if you know what it's about.«

I had no idea what he was talking about.

Amplifiers were fetched from a side room, which also served as a dressing room for bands. Beer on stage, cigarette out of the corner of my mouth.

Somehow, nobody was really interested in what I was playing. The self-promoters around me were too busy with themselves. Then, maybe half an hour later, the one everyone was eagerly waiting for arrived.

»Hey, let's see the list!« Jimmy leaned his guitar against the amplifier – break.

Herbert, whose snippy grin was framed by a little goatee, placed a notepad on the table. We could neatly see which pieces were available.

»I'll take that for twenty-five marks.«

»And me the twenty-two.«

»Have you got anything for eighteen?«

And so it went across the club. Herbert rummaged in his little bag, handed us what we wanted, and counted the money he had received. Then he neatly crossed the sold items off his list and said goodbye. He was undoubtedly the accountant among Hamburg's dealers.

Joints were being rolled and smoked everywhere, and the atmosphere was much more exuberant. We jammed until the early hours of the morning. Dude, that was cool.

»Hey Monty, can you recommend a bass teacher?«

»I can give you the phone number of Detlev Beier. He's the hottest jazz bassist in Hamburg.«

I came here almost every evening. Unfortunately, the whole thing didn't last long. Steve stopped, and nobody really knew why. That was the end of ›Let's Rock‹. After the rooms had been empty for a few months, they mutated into a Thai restaurant.

I have no idea how loud it was back then. Certainly not quiet, like most of the things I did at the time and in the years that followed. Nobody thought of any kind of ear protection, why should they? On the contrary: the louder the stereo system, the amplifier on stage, the band, the concert, or the disco was, the better. In a drugged state, anyway.

***

December 20, 2016. I called the ENT emergency department of a Hamburg hospital and was given an appointment with Dr. Rudolf Kempe for the next day. He, always with a flippant remark on his lips, suspiciously relaxed, got straight down to business.

»Which ear is affected?«

»Both«

»Then we can rule out a sudden hearing loss. A sudden loss of hearing in both ears at the same time is completely unknown. Let's go to the extreme and do a hearing test.«

No sooner said than done.

»You have a dip in the left ear at two kHz and in the right ear at three kHz. This is completely normal due to age. I can't tell you anything about your distorted hearing.« It seemed as he had never heard of such a phenomenon.

Dr. Kempe prescribed me a prophylactic medication, ›Prednisolon 20 mg‹ – cortisone. The fact that the distortion could not be diagnosed further made me wonder. I left with a bad feeling. I took the pills for ten days but noticed no improvement.

My next performance was scheduled for New Year's Eve. Final preparations for Christmas were currently in progress: Who was going to visit whom, when and where, getting the last presents and everything else that went with it. There was no reason for me to stay away from the festivities based on my suspicion.

On Christmas Day, fourteen of us sat around Petra's family table. We talked, ate, drank, unpacked, and commented, often several at the same time. My ears started to hurt.

The next day we set off in the car to my childhood home, which is a good six hundred kilometres away. Petra turned on the radio, and it sounded horrible.

»Please turn it off again, or at least turn it down.« It stayed off for the entire journey.

We stayed with Andreas Hunke, a fellow musician from the seventies, one of the few people from my hometown who credibly gives the impression that he is satisfied with the way his life has developed.

I spent the first evening doing more research on the internet. I discovered a clinic specializing in ear and hearing problems in Hamburg, which I contacted the next day.

»Unfortunately, we can't do anything for you. We are a clinic for private patients only.«

I realized how difficult it is to get medical assistance between Christmas and New Year. Many doctors have closed their practices, including my GP. It is an unfavourable time to develop health issues, especially when the time factor plays a not insignificant role.

In the evening, we met up with friends. The pub was small but full. It's just a sociable crowd down there. I felt comfortable, although the volume was immense. Everyone was chattering, and it got louder and louder as the alcohol level increased. The jukebox played non-stop. But my ears didn't hurt and I didn't notice the distortion.

One topic of the conversation was a concert from 1987 that I played with my first Hamburg jazz band at the Ellwangen Youth Centre.

***

Jazz? DEEP PURPLE and FRANK ZAPPA were my world. I couldn't do anything with jazz. But it certainly could help to sharpen my skills as a bass player. The decision was made, I called Detlev. On March 19, 1985, I set off for the first time.

»Come in,« he said, cigarette in hand, as he opened the door to his two-bedroom flat in Altona. I entered the small classroom. There were two chairs, a music stand, a stereo system, a sofa, a television, and a well-filled ashtray. It was undoubtedly the living room of a musician. My eyes fell on the only poster on the wall: JOACHIM KÜHN QUARTETT. I recognized Detlev from it. Only then did I realize the league this man was playing in. And I was just about to have my first lesson. I had been in Hamburg for less than two months, and it already had nothing to do with what I had experienced over the past twenty years. Since that day, ›Joachim Kühn Quartett‹ from 1982 has been on my record shelf.

I went to see him every Tuesday and practised for an average of six hours a day.

After a few months, he said: »By the way, a jazz club has opened in Gärtnerstraße, the ›Birdland‹. I play there next Saturday. Why don't you come by?«

It was October 26, 1985 when I entered a club like that for the first time, wow. I became a regular, and was soon playing in the house band at the weekly sessions. The blinkers of my youth began to come apart.

A few months later, I got a call asking if I would like to play with a well-known trombonist at ›Birdland‹.

The project was called ›ROLF TROUBNIKOFF & OASIS, special guest: ED KRÖGER‹. I didn't know Ed, Rolf, or any of my fellow musicians. There were no rehearsals, and I had to sight-read. This meant that I didn't get to see the sheets until the evening of the event. I don't know why, but after the concert Rolf, the pianist, came up to me. »Would you like to play in my quartet?«

I did.

At my request, Andreas organized a small tour for us in southern Germany. The day before the first gig, I was so tense that a feeling of paralysis spread through my left hand. I told myself it was probably just excitement and at the concert everything was fine; I was able to play.

The pressure was on me in two ways. Firstly, I was presenting myself for the first time in my old hometown after leaving, and secondly, I was miles away from the musical abilities of my colleagues. I had only recently gained experience. They, on the other hand, had studied jazz in Graz. One of the few cities in Europe whose university offered such a course at the time.

All in all, that was the first and one of the few top-class bands I played in over the years. Among other things, we won first place in the ›Youth Music Prize at the 21st Hannover Jazz Days‹ and the signs were good that something big could happen here.

Then came the news that brought it all to an abrupt end. Robert, our drummer, announced that he wanted to go to a monastery in Japan for a year. We couldn't find an adequate drummer for this time and after Robert's return, Rolf didn't want to play anymore. The bond between the two was torn.

***

On December 29, 2016, Petra and I drove back to Hamburg. One of the Christmas gifts that I received from her, was a book. The following evening, which was one of the few I spent alone during this time, I started to read it. Due to the increasing auditory distortion, I ensured that there was complete silence around me: no music, no television, nothing. I sat in my armchair, reading and enjoying the absolute silence.

It was the last time.

The Snake

If tinnitus occurs acutely, you should first keep calm. Tinnitus is not an emergency, but an urgent case. Therefore, you should waste no time and contact an ENT doctor or an ENT outpatient clinic in a hospital if you experience ringing in the ears. The earlier the treatment of tinnitus is started, the better the chances that it can be successfully treated.*

On the morning of December 31, 2016, I woke up and noticed two tones. Far away, soft, unthreatening. Already freaky, I didn't worry about it. The thought that there could be a connection to my distortion didn't even begin to cross my mind. It was like the ringing in your ears for a short time after a concert. The fact that I hadn't actually been to a concert was irrelevant. I was getting ready for my gig. New Year's Eve party in a hotel. I left at two o'clock. Playing time from eight to four in the morning. I went to bed at seven.

New Year 2017, I woke up. There were these whistling sounds. A very high-pitched one, slightly to the left at the top of my head, a lower one to the right behind my ear. Not dramatic, but persistent. I started observing them.

January 2, 2017, I woke up. The sounds were still there. They had become louder. I could no longer ignore them. This was followed by the aforementioned phone call with Dr. Kempe.

»There's nothing we can do. We no longer offer inpatient infusions. They have been proven to be ineffective. The same goes for Trental and Ginkgo. Consult a neurologist and try to distract yourself from the tinnitus. The best thing to do is to put headphones on …« The rest is history.

---

*Source (as at 01.10.2023): www.tinnitracks.com/de/tinnitus/akuter-chronischer-tinnitus
original language: german

Thus, the foundation for a constantly growing pressure within me was laid. It was the beginning of a journey of a different kind. An odyssey, the course of which I couldn't even begin to fathom.

***

I had unknowingly chosen my first Hamburg residence well. It was opposite the ›Fabrik‹ in Bahrenfelder Straße. Concerts took place here almost every day. From my room, I could see when the box office closed. That was the sign. I got up and went over there.

An old factory as a concert hall, pure big city. I was mostly on my own, and everywhere I looked, I saw bizarre people. Many of the bands, of whom I could enjoy the last half hour, came from the rock and jazz fusion scene. I only knew a few of them.

Don Cherry was playing. The first jazz band that captivated me. All styled. The musicians from this genre that I knew so far refused to do that.

»I want people to think I'm cool because of the notes I play.«

What a nonsense!

During a Birdland session, I once caused some displeasure.

»Why don't we do it so that only a few of you solo and the others in the next standard. Then it would be more varied.«

»You don't want to hear me soloing over *Blue Bossa*, do you?« Holy cow!

Don Cherry was more my style. That was show plus cool notes. In the late eighties, I experienced Miles Davis at the ›Fabrik‹. One of the most impressive concerts I have ever attended. It was pure show plus lots of really cool notes.

I moved in October 1985. A shared flat in Spaldingstraße became my second stop, St. Georg my home for two and a half years. It was a seedier place than Altona: central station, drug dealing, street prostitution.

My room furnishings consisted mainly of bulky rubbish. It was still the time when people used to put their old furnitures out on the curb every few months. We would then go on evening forays declared as a shared flat outing. Whatever seemed useful was packed up. I had nailed together my bed frame from old slats.

One afternoon, I was a guest at a garden party.

»I heard you're a musician,« the host said cheerfully as he sat down next to me.

»I have guests over in the summer and I also play a bit of guitar. Would you like to bring your instrument sometime? I'm sure it would be great fun.«

»Why not, I heard you're a carpenter. I could do with a new bed.«

Within a few seconds, his expression changed from ›beaming with joy‹ to ›completely serious‹.

»Well, I would have to charge at least thirty-five Marks per hour for that.«

It was a revealing afternoon, I never played there.

At the age of twenty-three, I experienced my second attack of gout. I limped off in search of a doctor and found Dr. Hans Pielke on Lange Reihe, a street near the central station. He was the only one in the region who had consultation hours on a Wednesday afternoon. The way he removed a drug addict from his toilet was unmistakable and impressive. This time the results of the blood test were clear – everything was above the limit.

Gout continued to bother me from then on. When necessary, it was treated by taking Allopurinol, a medication to lower the purine levels in the blood. One side effect was a considerable itching sensation on the tip of the pecker. Enjoy scratching, is all I can say.

***

When I moved back to Altona in 1988, there was no reason for me to look for another GP. Although it was time-consuming to make an appointment, the trust relationship I had built was worth it to me.

On January 3, 2017, I set out on my way. I entered the practice and was greeted by his receptionist wearing a headscarf and in good spirits at the front desk.

»Good morning, Mr. Kolb.« She had an excellent capacity for remembering names.

»I know I don't have an appointment, but I really need to speak to the doctor.«

»No problem, please have a seat in the waiting room.«

The practice isn't very big. There are a few seats in the waiting area, which seem to be randomly arranged and are rarely all occupied. Outdated journals and magazines are scattered on the table.

My gaze kept wandering back to the door of the doctor's office, hoping that it would open soon. After a few minutes, it did.

»I need to confirm the colleague's statements. Unfortunately, the human brain works that way, similar to pain memory. The first five to ten days are crucial. If the tinnitus is still there after that, it will be difficult.«

Countless phone calls were dominating the following days. First, I spoke with an employee of the Eppendorf Tinnitus Center.

»At the moment, we can't do anything for you, as we only deal with chronic cases here.«

The second sentence was slightly more encouraging: »You now need to see a neurologist, an orthopaedist, an

ENT doctor, and a dentist to investigate possible causes. This is a prerequisite for further measures.«

»I can offer you an appointment in ten days,« said an employee of Dr. Hermann Kraft on the other end of the line. I had been a patient at his ENT practice for several years.

»But I've had tinnitus for four days. We need to act quickly.«

»I'm sorry, we're fully booked. I can't offer you an earlier appointment.« The old girl stood her ground.

I found another ENT doctor in my area. The next morning at seven o'clock, I waited with three other patients in front of his office for an emergency appointment. Amazingly fast, I found myself in a treatment room.

»Then let's do a hearing test to see in which frequency range your sounds are located.«

In my opinion, the test conducted by an assistant was amateurish and did not lead to any real results. Thanks to my training, I was able to identify them by myself. The higher one was a slightly too low 'G' at twelve thousand hertz. A tone much higher than the highest one of a piccolo flute, as we know it from marching bands. When hearing decreases in this frequency range, which is normal from the age of fifty, glass begins to sound like plastic and the noise of water flushing down the toilet no longer has the same freshness. The second tone was about an octave lower, at six thousand hertz. A range that, with a bit of luck, you can hear well into old age. At the latest, when it's gone, everyone in the house can hear what you're watching on TV.

I eventually sat in the doctor's consultation room. He was young and had an arrogant, know-it-all, unsympathetic demeanour.

»There's nothing you can do for tinnitus, you'll have to live with it. There are so-called ›noisers‹ that you can use to try to eliminate it from your perception. Otherwise, I recommend self-help groups. I can give you prescriptions for Ginkgo and Magnesium, if you'd like, but it won't help much. I can't say anything about your hearing distortion.« I got the Magnesium, but not the Ginkgo.

The following morning, I visited a neurologist. I had surprisingly managed to get an appointment quickly. Generally speaking, you will have to wait up to three months for an examination. His introductory conversation was unique: »I don't think there's anything I can do for you. It's always the same. When doctors from other specialities are stumped, they send the patients to the neurologist to fix it.«

After that was cleared up, there was the examination. Electrodes were attached to my temples and different sound sources were played into my ears through headphones. I felt like a monkey in an experimental laboratory as my brain waves were measured, and as predicted, no irregularities were detected. Afterwards, I went to the front desk to schedule an appointment for an ultrasound examination.

The next day, I was sitting with Dr. Albert Kosnick, an orthopaedist. I was also able to tell him about severe pain in my right knee and problems in my left arm. I had been experiencing these issues since crossing the Atlantic. My hope was that there was a connection here and that the tinnitus would disappear with successful treatment of the symptoms.

»Unfortunately, I cannot do anything for your ear troubles. You can cool your arm with pads. For the knee, I will give you a referral for an MRI. Let me know when you have the results.«

What was remarkable about the examination was that Dr. Kosnick didn't touch me once. Throughout the entire time, he remained glued to his chair.

Over the past few years, I have had several dentists for various reasons. During my time off in the alps, a piece of one of my molars broke off. It was not easy to find a time in the mountains when there was a network connection for my mobile phone. I did not know Dr. Stefan Hartung at the time, but I was able to schedule an appointment with him for right after my return. Now, I consulted him for the second time.

»I cannot find anything unusual with your teeth. You tend to grind your teeth and your jaw is tense. Do you have a dental splint for your upper jaw? How old is it?«

»It's probably about ten years old.«

»Then let's get another one made for the lower jaw. Chiropractic care may be able to help with tinnitus.«

Meanwhile, the ten days had passed, and I was sitting in the waiting room at Dr. Kraft's office. My sounds had become louder and louder. I was picked up by a young lady in white clothing who conducted a hearing test. She reminded me of Mirjam, but that was a long time ago.

»Mr. Kolb, we couldn't find anything. There are hardly any options for tinnitus, and I can't say anything about your distortion. I'll give you a referral for an MRI scan of your head. We'll see each other again after that.« The conversation with Dr. Kraft was one of the shorter ones.

I started wondering what the point of all these hearing tests was. What are they supposed to see? I was able to organize both MRI appointments at two different radiology practices in good time. I was just as lucky in this respect as I was with the neurologist.

***

I have always enjoyed cooking, and most of the time it was also to the taste of those present. Jens lived a floor above our shared flat in Spaldingstraße. Sometimes he would come over and get spoiled by my Swabian cuisine. One evening, the phone rang; a friend of his had called.

»Hey, I'm Mirjam. I just got your number from Jens. I work here at the ›Springbrunnen‹ on Borgweg. We're urgently looking for someone to work in the kitchen. Are you interested?«

»Most definitely, when should I start?«

»It would be cool if you could come over right away, our chef hasn't turned up.«

What can I say, I set off. You didn't have to be a trained chef for this job. It was enough to know just how to heat water and how big a portion should be.

Running Up That Hill by KATE BUSH was playing through the speakers when I saw Mirjam for the first time. She was my age and incredibly cute. I had an instant crush on her. We got closer, fell in love and she became my first girlfriend in Hamburg. However, there was also Martin, the man at the bar. He was quite a bit older and also interested in Mirjam. Unfortunately, she wasn't sure who she liked more. Sometimes she leaned towards him, sometimes towards me, and the whole thing turned into a disaster.

Martin didn't miss a chance to let me know when he had spent the night with her. I was completely overwhelmed by this love triangle.

The most difficult part was when the three of us were working a shift together. Martin at the counter, me in the kitchen and Mirjam in between. There was this classic serving hatch where I put the finished dishes so that Mirjam could bring them to the guests. In those moments, I always saw the two of them flirting in front of the taps. One evening, it became too much for me and my emotions burst out in the form of a crying fit, something I hadn't experienced in a long time. A few days later, I ended the relationship and quit. Mirjam was with Martin for several years afterwards.

It was the last time I had a crying fit. In the many years that followed, I naturally had to endure difficult situations and breakups, but tears didn't come to me on those occasions anymore.

I actually see myself as a closeted hippie who was born ten years too late. But I'm sure that free love would have driven me out of my mind.

***

In the last week of January 2017, the appointments for MRI scans took place. Neither could provide any results regarding a possible cause. I picked up the dental splint and the neurologist completed his ultrasound examination. I was perfectly healthy, my distorted hearing perception was a phenomenon, and because of the ringing in my ears, I was repeatedly referred to self-help groups.

I was made aware of treatment options such as noisers and chiropractic care. Unfortunately, a sentence in the way of ›I don't know of a solution or possibility myself, but I will ask my colleagues if anything is known‹ was never uttered.

On the contrary, some doctors made me feel like I should just leave and not waste their time any further. I felt completely abandoned. With Petra's help, I had to painstakingly research all the other treatment options by myself.

That was the phase in which I realized that this was no game. The tinnitus became more overpowering every day and meant that I could no longer sleep well. More and more often, I lay awake in bed for hours at night. A snake had wrapped itself around me, slowly but surely tightening its grip, and a feeling of despair began to spread.

Intratympanic Steroid Therapy

Tinnitus is a hearing experience perceived in one or both ears without an external sound source. It is based on a disturbance of the auditory function. The auditory impression of tinnitus does not usually have any relation to the sound in the patient's environment. The type of apparent noise is very varied: the auditory impressions are described as humming, whistling, hissing, crackling or knocking. The intensity of the sound can be constant, but it can also have a fluctuating or even rhythmic-pulsating character. However, it does not always resemble a sound from the real acoustic environment. Tinnitus must also be clearly distinguished from auditory hallucinations, known as acoasmia.

Tinnitus can also be artificially induced in the majority of people with good hearing, simply by spending a few minutes in a noiseless, soundproof cabin. Possible explanations for this include an unaccustomed influence on the normal loudness tuning in the auditory brain or a masking of a weak tinnitus that was already present but hidden by the normal environmental noise.

Tinnitus is often divided into different degrees of severity. Biesinger defines four degrees of severity:

- *Grade I: The tinnitus hardly bothers the person affected. Despite the ringing in the ears, there is no suffering.*
- *Grade II: Those affected can still cope with their everyday life without any major negative consequences. However, the tinnitus is experienced as stressful in certain situations or under stress.*

- *Grade III: There are permanent impairments to quality of life and occupational performance. Emotional, physical and cognitive disorders are to be expected. The affected persons are still able to work.*
- *Grade IV: Complete decompensation: those affected are severely impaired both professionally and privately; inability to work, suicidal thoughts or attempts.*

From Grade III, one speaks of decompensated tinnitus.*

***

The fourth week began. The clock was ticking mercilessly. Still, the only medical advice was to distract myself by listening to music. I did all the gigs that were on my calendar. It was a disaster.

Sometimes I worked on stage with in-ear monitoring, headphones that are custom-fit to my ear canals. It was only now that I realized I had been perceiving this signal distorted for months. Our band leader had tried in vain to figure out what was causing it.

»The aux path of the mixing console is faulty.«

»I can't detect anything, it sounds completely normal to me.« He shrugged his shoulders.

And I thought, what can you hear anyway?

The distortion was now also present in conversations, varying in intensity from voice to voice. It was more noticeable at higher volumes, but also audible at lower levels. The tinnitus still consisted of the two tones.

I got tired early, slept restlessly, and often lay wide awake in bed after only a few hours. The ringing in my ears was too loud to fall asleep again. On top of that, due to the un-

---

*Source: (as at 01.10.2023): https://de.wikipedia.org/wiki/Tinnitus
original language: german

successfulness of my previous activities, the perceived lack of support from doctors, and the growing fear that I was running out of time, I could hardly breathe freely anymore. The noose tightened further and further.

Without any prospect that this situation could change for the better in the foreseeable future or at all, they came. Thoughts that everyone knows. They weren't new to me either. But in the ever-increasing hopelessness, they were massive and unfamiliar concrete.

I began to organize my life: what needed to be done to leave behind as little inconvenience for posterity as possible. I would have to cancel insurances, sell instruments, and much more.

Elli, my cat, hopped onto the bed. Originally, I had two. Unfortunately, I had to put Piet to sleep some time ago, but more on that later. Elli looked at me, settled by my side, and took me out of this destructive world. I started to scratch her tummy, which she enjoyed with purring. She should never end up in a shelter again.

At two o'clock I got up, went to the computer, worked or listened to soft music. I tried to find a balance that didn't make it sound too horrible and at the same time softened the tinnitus. But being carried away by it and going on a journey together was over.

Sometimes, I would have the TV on quietly, and do finger exercises on the bass without an amplifier. All of this helped distract me, pass the time. But the depression had a firm grip on me.

***

Two o'clock in the morning. A year after I arrived in Hamburg, that was the time when I would receive approving looks at sessions. I took advantage of pretty much every opportunity that presented itself and was out almost every evening.

»Dude, that's really cool what you're playing.«

I hadn't even noticed how practising every day was already making itself felt.

The shared flat life and the new environment soon became normal. The briquettes burned in the oven, slowly and pleasantly warming the high ceilings of the old building with their soot-blackened stucco. I sat on the sofa, flipping through a city magazine and reading the ad: *Cover band looking for bass player, approx. 750 marks a month.* An unimaginable sum for me at that time. I applied and was handed a cassette.

In the following days, I spent hours in front of my tape deck, fast-forwarding and rewinding, bar by bar. It took ages to pick out the bass from the sometimes poor quality, especially as I had never done anything like this before. But it was good practice. I wasn't just training my ears; I got a feel for the structure of pop songs and how the bass is used in them. I started to like pop music.

With a mixture of nervousness and self-confidence, I entered the rehearsal room. We played the songs, and here too I noticed a positive surprise. I went home in a good mood, even though I knew I wasn't the only one they met.

A few days later I got the call. »We would be happy if you join us.«

I once again entered a world unknown to me and bought a few records to familiarize myself with the style. Among them was ›Like A Virgin‹ by Madonna. *Into the Groove* was one of the most popular songs in Hamburg's nightclubs. It's quite conceivable that I bought it only because of the cover, as a colleague suggested me years later.

The era of ›Stock Aitken Waterman‹, a team of producers responsible for Rick Astley and Kylie Minogue, began. They created a sound that would dominate the pop-disco scene for several years. The computer made its entrance in the form of the ›Atari 1040‹: Revolution! However, it would still take some time before we used one. Thanks to my piano skills, I was able to play the synth basses live and bought me a ›Casio AZ-1‹. One of these futuristic-looking strap-on synths.

One of our regular venues was the ›Bierdorf‹ on Mittel-weg. There were many steps down into a usually completely overcrowded cauldron. Once, I didn't feel well. I was suffering from a cold, a slight fever and aching limbs. The smoky and sweat-soaked air finished the job. During the last song before the break, I realized that it was only a matter of minutes before something wanted to come out of my throat.

The song was over. I put the bass in the corner, fought my way through the crowd, reached the toilet and ran into a cubicle. Door closed, lid up, head over it and off I went. Not five seconds too soon. I rinsed my mouth out, went to the bar, ordered a new beer, and made it back in time for the next set.

That was rock'n'roll.

***

Dr. Pielke wrote me a prescription for physiotherapy. I accepted it together with a small box.

»I have a sample pack of Ginkgo here. Why don't you give it a try? You should see it as a course and take it daily for at least four months.«

As long as it doesn't do any harm, I don't care. I started taking it without believing in it.

I visited another orthopaedist who, unlike my first experience, actively treated me. He put his hands on me and adjusted the upper cervical vertebrae. At least it cracked. Unfortunately, my hope that the knee and arm pain could be related to the tinnitus was not confirmed by him either. That would have been too good to be true.

I had no experience with alternatives to conventional medicine. The first one I decided to try was osteopathy. Maria Krempel's practice was just a few minutes' walk away from my flat. The street noise became increasingly unbearable, and the journey to her was torture.

She was around my age and of slender build. With a reserved demeanour that could almost be described as submissive, she led me into her sparsely furnished room. Located in a shared practice, it was just big enough to walk around the centrally positioned treatment table in a relaxed manner. There was also a small table with two chairs in front of the window.

I was surprised by the strength of her hands when she began adjusting joints, massaging, and bringing my body into balance. Over the next two weeks, I was with her four times. The treatment, which I paid for entirely out of pocket, felt good, but it didn't provide noticeable relief.

At least not for the moment.

When I got home from Mrs. Krempel's on February 4, there was an email from Petra in my mailbox with a link:
>Take a look at this. It's just like you always describe it.<

Dysacusis (hearing distortion). Dysacusis refers to the condition of hearing distortion. The usual auditory impression suddenly changes. Those affected hear sounds and speech distorted, echoing and screeching in their ears. The condition of dysacusis is often associated with hyperacusis and/or the symptom >pressure in the ear<.

Like hyperacusis, hearing distortion is an emergency and alarm signal that comes from overstrained and overloaded auditory cells. It can affect hearing as a whole or >only< individual frequencies. […]

Dysacusis, along with pressure in the ear and hyperacusis, can be an alarm signal that is at the beginning of inner ear overload or can occur intermittently or continuously as part of a progressive inner ear overload.[*]

Dysacusis, suddenly we were making progress. I was not affected by the hyperacusis and the pressure in my ear that were also described. Not yet.

While reading through the article, I came across the possibility of laser therapy for tinnitus and that there is an alternative practitioner in Hamburg who offers it. This is remarkable, as there are only a few such practices in Germany, and sufferers often have to travel several hundred kilometres to be treated in this way.

Another link in the email led me to Dr. Ernst Meinard's website, an ENT specialist, where a colleague of Petra's had treated her tinnitus with intratympanic steroid therapy, or ITS for short.

This email had a huge impact. The fact that I finally knew what was happening with my ears and the newfound possibilities gave me hope. The snake's pressure gave way, albeit only slightly. To this day, I cannot understand why these search results did not come up in my own research and why none of the previous specialists I had consulted so far had mentioned the term ›dysacusis‹ or ›intratympanic steroid therapy‹, let alone the ›low level laser therapy‹. But that's how it was.

Small insertion: A few weeks after reading about the ITS, I found myself back on Dr. Kraft's website. I have no idea why, probably just didn't have anything better to do. I couldn't believe my eyes. By now, he was offering it too. It was crazy; at the beginning of the year he had no idea how to help me.

---

[*] *Source: http://dasgesundeohr.de,* but the site is no longer online
original language: german

I called Dr. Meinard's practice and made an appointment. A few days later, I sat opposite him. What a nice man! He looked youthful and had this warm-hearted way that immediately made me feel good. A hit with the ladies for sure! He was the first doctor I consulted who was familiar with the phenomenon of distorted hearing and the term dysacusis.

»How long have you had your problems?«

»The distortion eight weeks, the tinnitus six.«

»Then it's a bit late for the ITS, but we can still try.«

»Are there any other options?«

»In the past, treatment was with infusions, but that is no longer offered here.«

»What about Ginkgo or acupuncture?«

»Acupuncture can be utilized, but only within the first few weeks after the symptoms appear in conjunction with ITS. Ginkgo is a placebo.«

»Have you heard of laser therapy?«

»You'd better keep your hands off it.«

He referred to studies on both Ginkgo and low level laser therapy.

»Mr. Kolb, tinnitus, dysacusis, hyperacusis and Menière's disease are symptoms of inner ear overload. You need to give your inner ear the opportunity to regenerate. If you have a sprained ankle, you wouldn't run a marathon. You put your leg up and rest it. You should avoid any form of loud noise, go into a quiet environment, and use ear protection. However, you shouldn't completely shut off your ears.«

I had already read about overstraining and resting on Robert Kroll's website, the alternative practitioner for laser therapy. Even though it was the only point they both agreed on, it made it all the more plausible for me. So after this conversation, I cancelled all my gigs until the end of May. That was the time when I hoped to be healthy again.

On one hand, this conversation was positive because it was the first time a treatment specific to tinnitus could begin. On the other hand, I was made aware that time was already working greatly against me.

»I must inform you that this is not covered by health insurance. You will have to pay for the ITS and the serum required for the treatment yourself.«

It was unexpected, but there was no way around it. The treatment consisted of five injections per ear, alternating over ten days. Initially, Dr. Meinard placed a band soaked in anaesthetic in front of my eardrum. Just like at the dentist, we had to wait for it to take effect. The thought of having a cortisone mixture injected through my eardrum with a syringe made me sit up slightly tense in the chair.

»You must remain completely still now. It's important that you don't speak afterwards, so that the serum stays inside. You may feel a bit dizzy for a few seconds. Please give a hand signal when it's over. A thumbs up is best. You will then be taken to the relaxation room. Here you will lie on your side for ten minutes with the treated ear facing upwards. Then you can leave.«

The injection was unpleasant, but not painful. Even after the first injection, my tones started to move around in my head. Until that day, they had been firmly anchored and hadn't moved a millimetre since they appeared. Dr. Meinard interpreted this as a good sign. All medical disciplines agree that tinnitus that is in motion has better chances of being cured. What was unpleasant was that extreme sensitivity to all kinds of noises developed.

»This may occur as a side effect of the treatment, but it subsides over time.«

Unfortunately, the opposite was the case. After just a few days, the flick of a light switch caused pain in my ears.

To make matters worse, I had to cope with an extreme noise level at home. The flat below me was being renovated due to a change of tenant and the work took six weeks. Sometimes the jackhammer started at seven in the morning. There were also countless roadworks in Altona, as the city of Hamburg was of the opinion that all the pipes had to be replaced right now. And finally, the Große Bergstraße, a pedestrian zone and shopping mile in my immediate neighbourhood, was being resurfaced. For me, this meant that I had to wear hearing protection as soon as I left my flat. Even when I stepped onto the balcony.

Inside my flat, I used construction site earmuffs when doing housework such as washing dishes or vacuuming – even brushing my teeth: a relic from the old days. I got it in 1987 when I was working as a musician at ›Deutsches Schauspielhaus‹ in Hamburg. I sometimes keep objects like this for nostalgic reasons. I would never have thought that thirty years later it would become an important utensil for me.

When I was on the phone, I held the receiver away from my ear, with the speaker facing the floor. Sometimes I didn't answer my cell phone at all, and I limited my television viewing to one movie in the evening. I stopped listening to music completely, even if only quietly in the background. With the exception of outside noise sources, my flat was dead quiet.

Hello, hyperacusis.

***

The shared flat in Spaldingstraße was a functional flat share. Everyone lived their lives, did their own thing, and occasionally there was a party. For one basic problem – how do we do the washing up? – there was an incredibly simple, but super working rule: always in alphabetical order. You did the job and the ball was in the next person's court.

People around me often said: »Well, you can do the dishes if there are only two plates.«

That's absolutely true, but it never happened. The impulse to get to work always came when a mountain of dishes had accumulated that was worth doing. There was never any trouble or a flatmate had to be reminded. All in all, it's still a phenomenon for me today.

Once again, I had fulfilled my part of the agreement. While drying my hands, the phone rang. I walked down the long, narrow corridor to our communication station and picked up. Detlev was on the other end.

»I've got a job at the theatre and need a sub, would you be up for it? You'd do the rehearsals and performances that I can't.«

»Ey cool.«

»Are you up for it?« It was only then that I heard the seriousness in his voice. This wasn't a joke. This was an offer to work as a sub for one of the best bassists in town.

»Yes, of course,« I replied meekly.

I sat down on the sofa in my room. Did that really happen? It wasn't long before it rang again.

»It's about a play that Peter Zadek is directing – ›Andi‹. The music is by Peer Raben. The rehearsals are taking place at a rehearsal stage in Billstedt. You'll need to take over next week, I'll bring you the sheets right away.«

A few days later I set off, it was amazing. There they all were. Ulrich Tukur, Uwe Bohm, Susanne Lothar, ›Ekel Alfred‹ Heinz Schubert. And me in the middle of it all. The rehearsals for ›Andi‹ lasted three months. It was based on a true story about vigilante justice: a kiosk owner shot a rioting sixteen-year-old who was tampering with his car.

Peter Zadek let his actors improvise for the first few weeks. There were days when he developed a single scene with two of them. At the same time, it was important to him that all the actors were always present. That's how I ended up playing pinball with Eva Mattes. Christian Redl came up to me: »Say, can you teach me a bit of harmony theory?«

Where am I actually here?

There was a second band, the EINSTÜRZENDE NEUBAUTEN. While mine was responsible for accompanying singing actors, the Neubauten had several performances during the three-hour play. There was always full energy. It never seemed like they were in rehearsal mode and playing at half power. It was very impressive, but also took place at an incredible volume. The entire staff around Peter Zadek had left the hall during these ten-minute performances. We were given our construction site earmuffs and avoiding staying there longer than necessary.

Later, during the shows, earplugs were distributed for free in the theatre's foyer and a notice was put up highlighting the noise level and disclaiming any liability for health damage from exposure to loud noise.

***

The longer the ITS lasted, the more my tinnitus shifted to the back of my head, which was much more pleasant.

The two clearly localizable tones were joined by a slight, high-frequency noise. For a short time, my sounds were quiet immediately after getting up and only increased during the course of the day. Then they were loud again in the morning. This changeability is confirmed as known by most doctors.

I took note of all this. However, as I now also had the hypersensitivity for any kind of noises, the hearing distortion remained unaffected, and the tinnitus did not become any quieter in the long term, my tendency towards depression increased.

After the injections, the further course of treatment included three weeks of medication with a blood circulation stimulant. I started taking ›Trental 400 mg‹. Within a few days, the volume in my head swelled to an unimaginable level. It was filled with a wide variety of noises in combination with countless, sometimes highly aggressive sounds.

Petra was with me. I laid my head in her lap, put on my headphones for the first time in months, and listened to the music as loud as necessary to escape the noise, at least a little bit.

The nights were pure torture. My negative thoughts about the meaning of life reached their peak. Why should I suffer to the end of my days just so that others might not feel quite so shitty for the moment? I went through the lists more and more meticulously. What options are available to me to end this? And what the hell am I going to do with Elli?

I found these mind games less and less destructive. On the contrary, I even became more relaxed. In hindsight, I think the fact that I was increasingly allowing myself to accept this possibility as completely okay was decisive for this.

After that weekend, I stopped taking the Trental.

»A strong increase in ringing in the ears due to the medication is not unknown. Your condition should have normalized again in a few days.«

Dr. Meinard was right. That was certainly one of the reasons why it remained just a mind game. I looked into the abyss, but didn't jump.

First Experiences with Health Insurance Fund

So far, I have come across three theories on the subject of chronic tinnitus.

Firstly, three months is the time limit most frequently propagated by conventional medicine for considering tinnitus as chronic. Another – secondly – states that the period from the fourth to the sixth month is to be regarded as an intermediate stage before it becomes chronic. The version that – thirdly – this state is reached after one year is less common.

It was only much later that I was informed that the main purpose of setting such a time limit is to change the type of treatment. For example, you can then apply for rehab or go to one of those clinics that only treat chronic patients. This does not necessarily mean that the fat lady has sung.

The ringing in my ears had now been bothering me for almost two months, the distortion for longer, and I was getting closer and closer to the ominous three months. My anxiety became more and more powerful every day, and I was constantly on the run. Just don't listen. If you listen, that's it. The snake looked me in the eye, lambent.

I started drinking chamomile or peppermint tea in the evening and taking valerian tablets in the hope that this would help me to fall asleep or sleep through the night. I believe that both were helpful.

After just a few days, I noticed a pleasant feeling in my legs that spread a good hour after taking the valerian. This became the sign for me that I would soon fall asleep.

However, this depended on the brand. I tested different products, some gave me nightmares. At least they stopped again when I switched back to my original variety.

I left my flat less and less. Only for doctor's appointments, shopping, or to get half an hour of fresh air. Wearing the ear protection was both, a blessing and a curse. I was afraid to use it because it made the tinnitus more direct and even louder, but I was protected from the surrounding noise. Back at home, I literally tore it out of my ears to get some distance again.

My upper wisdom teeth were extracted a long time ago. The one in my lower right jaw was chiselled out fifteen years ago by oral surgeon Dr. Sigurd Mansfeld, now an elderly gentleman with his sights firmly set on retirement. Since then, I have consulted him irregularly to have the position of the remaining one checked. I remembered this and got a glimmer of hope that this might be the root of the problem.

»When I compare the x-ray with the one taken three years ago, I can't see any difference. The tooth hasn't moved. You have a very tense jaw. I write you a prescription for TMJ.«

For the TMJ treatment, I went to the same practice that I had already visited for physiotherapy. It was the same as a few weeks ago. The first treatment, which was carried out by a female member of staff, was as prescribed. After that, I came under the care of a male member of staff who was following his own ideas. As I couldn't judge to what extent his method helped the cause, I let him continue.

When Dr. Mansfeld wrote me a second prescription a few weeks later, I went to another practice. Here I was treated exactly as prescribed. Ultimately, however, it didn't matter as neither version brought any improvement.

Dr. Pielke was very helpful and supported me with all my concerns during this difficult time. I would therefore consider him a good GP. He offered me sick leave at an early stage. As I was firmly convinced that this would be of no use to me as a freelance musician, I thankfully declined.

Over the decades, I have always fulfilled my musical obligations. Even under conditions that can be described as questionable from a health point of view. For example, I was carted to gigs on crutches with acute gout attacks or played ten gigs in two weeks with bronchitis.

Rather by chance, I came across a news item that said that freelancers are entitled to sick pay amounting to seventy percent of their income from the seventh week onwards. In my case, the income was the amount I had registered with the artists' social security fund. At the end of February 2017, at the tender age of fifty-four, I took sick leave for the first time in my life. Completely unfamiliar with this process, I went to the nearest branch of my health insurance fund to hand in this yellow slip of paper in person to one of the clerks.

»You are entitled to sick pay for up to seventy-two weeks. You will be informed of the amount in writing.«

That sounded surprisingly uncomplicated, and I was overcome with a feeling of security. Of course, I hoped that I wouldn't have to claim the sickness benefit for long, but now I had a safety net in case my condition remained like this for longer. At least that's what I thought. The fact that I didn't receive any continued pay for the first six weeks was self-explanatory.

***

Safety nets didn't play a role in my life until now. That was far too bourgeois for me. If I had worried about safety nets, I wouldn't have become a musician.

By the end of the eighties, hard rock had reached an incredible level of popularity from today's perspective. Bands like WHITESNAKE and GUNS N' ROSES dominated the charts. MTV was the hip channel, ›Headbanger's Ballroom‹ was the must-see show, and in the rock clubs of Hamburg, videos were playing all evening.

In an Altona pub, I met Gunnar. At the time, he was the guitarist for ZED YAGO, a successful heavy metal band from Hamburg. However, he wasn't happy there. Slightly younger than me, he was one of the few people who crossed my path who were kissed by talent in a way that I could only dream of.

During our first boozy evening, we decided to meet up with a drummer for a private jam. This was not allowed by his record company. A friendship developed that heralded the most intense and exciting time of my entire musical life.

Gunnar soon left ZED YAGO and we formed LONE AGE. The second band in my career, consistently filled with incredibly talented musicians. However, I realized that was not the most important thing.

I also quit my Top-40 band so that I could concentrate fully on our project and went looking for a job. I came across an advertisement in the Altonaer Wochenblatt: *McDonald's branch looking for night cleaner.*

Since I had become a night owl, going to bed around six in the morning on average and then sleeping until noon, this job seemed suitable to me. It would also look very good on the CV of a future rock star: ›*Was a night cleaner at McDonald's*‹, or even better: ›*From night cleaner to rock star*‹.

I applied and was invited to work. Alongside my colleague, a Black African whose name I can't remember, I started to dismantle the grills. The cleaning agent we had at our disposal transported the thickest layers of fat into nirvana without much effort. Afterwards, the kitchen, including the dining area, was thoroughly scrubbed, and it was home to bed.

Despite wearing sturdy rubber gloves, I found that my hands were useless the day after a shift. Active music-making or practising was hardly possible. I think it was due to both the cleaning agent and the very hot water. I informed the branch manager that I could no longer do this work. He then offered me the chance to work in sales during the day. I accepted and spent the next year and a half at the drive-in counter on Stresemannstraße 354, selling countless burgers and milkshakes.

During this time, Gunnar and I wrote songs with Keith, our singer, and the three of us made ours rounds of the bars. Cocaine made its way into my life. Sometimes we went straight from the front door into a back room and found the lines already spread out on the table. Can you get any more cliché? I was naturally curious and didn't need to be asked twice, but soon realized that this drug didn't turn me on at all. I was more into hallucinogens, I wanted to fly away. Cocaine was just a pick-me-up for me and simply too expensive for that.

Through Gunnar's contacts, we quickly got in touch with a major publisher and through them with record labels. At that time, there were still many of the so-called major companies. Due to their financial resources, they had the power to push an act to the top through elaborate record and video productions as well as large advertising budgets. But they could also make an act disappear into insignificance. There were stories circulating about bands being signed by such companies and then nothing being done with them; they were thus hung out to dry. The purpose was to eliminate potential rivals of their top-selling artists from the market. You had to be careful who you signed up with.

We met with important representatives of such companies who were responsible for purchasing. To cut a long story short, I didn't get the impression that these people knew anything about music. I rather came to the conclusion that they were businessmen who didn't care whether they were launching a new detergent or a band into the market. ›Marketing Concept‹ was the magic word. It was never about the content, the music, but about the packaging. The development of a concept that would persuade a potential buyer to purchase a product. That was sobering. As we never came to an agreement, we produced a CD ourselves together with ›Studio M‹ near Hildesheim. The whole thing dragged on for three years, which wore us down. At the end of the day, LONE AGE no longer existed by the time the CD was released. In the second half of the nineties, Gunnar and I lost touch.

***

In January 2016, I received the news that Keith, our singer at the time, had passed away at the age of 53. From a sobering perspective, it wasn't surprising. He was one of the few in my circle who had truly lived the ›sex & drugs & rock'n'roll‹ lifestyle. His death was the reason that Gunnar and I got in touch again after almost twenty years. Over the summer, we sat together in Petra's garden. The grill was heating up and while we were chatting, he mentioned in an aside: »I've had tinnitus since then, and it's only got louder over the years.«

»Since 1992? Don't fuck around.«

»We were rehearsing and when I drove home, it started ringing. I don't remember why, but we rehearsed there for five consecutive days.«

I took note of this, but didn't give much thought to what it meant.

This incident keeps coming back to my mind. It shows

how little all of us engage with our surroundings and our fellow human beings. Essentially, everyone is primarily preoccupied with his own little world. That's why I can understand that people in my circle are reserved or don't react at all when they hear about my tinnitus. Not to mention the hearing distortion and hypersensitivity.

But it's also revealing to see who reaches out during tough times and who never does. I at least took clear note of this and drew my conclusions from it. In other words, there are people I no longer need to have anything to do with.

Up until the time I experienced my own tinnitus, Gunnar was the only person among those close to me who I knew was suffering from it. He wasn't the only one who kept it to himself back then. Musicians hardly ever talk about ear problems. The fear of not being called for jobs anymore is too prevalent for many. I never thought about whether it could be a disadvantage to talk about it. On the contrary, I was open about it so that it would be understood why I don't want to go to a loud pub or stand right next to the cymbals of the drum kit.

Now I learned, that a surprisingly large number of colleagues and people I have crossed paths with have been living with one or more noises in their heads for many years.

They suffer in silence.

***

I have been advised of the possibility of psychotherapy several times over the past few months. I had always kept this option in the back of my mind. The incidents of the past weeks, especially the sleepless nights, have prompted me to tackle the issue now. Dr. Meinard and Dr. Pielke supported me in this.

On March 1, 2017, I set out.

»What can I do for you?« This specimen of a case-worker had definitely stopped looking interested.

»I'd like to find out about the possibility of psycho-therapy. How the application process works and so on.«

»Is there a specific reason?«

»I've been suffering from tinnitus since the beginning of the year.«

Only now did he look at me.

»I've had it for two years too. I've even thought about jumping off a bridge. I put on headphones at home and listen to music. Many don't believe it, but it helps me.«

He seemed disillusioned as he said that, and I didn't get the impression that it was true. But it led to a pleasant conversation that wasn't at all destructive. We both took the opportunity to exchange our thoughts with a fellow sufferer.

»I'll give you the link to a database of therapists.«

Back at home, I typed ›psych-info.de‹ into the browser's address bar and worked my way through the countless results that were displayed in my vicinity. I came across the profile of psychologist Frauke Glaser, where tinnitus was listed as a treatment focus. As luck would have it, a telephone consultation was possible for the same day.

Mrs. Glaser answered. I was prepared to be cut off with the excuse that there was currently no availability. We talked for twenty minutes.

»I know you're going through a very difficult time. I myself have been suffering from tinnitus for some time. Are you listening to music right now?«

In the background, a meditation CD was playing, which I had discovered in a one-euro shop a few days ago.

»Could you perhaps turn that off?« I complied with her request and was surprised when she said: »It's more pleasant now.«

The music was barely audible to me, and unpleasant for her through the phone? I don't know, as she took so much time with every caller, but her empathy made me feel a lot more relaxed during the call.

»I can see that you need therapy as soon as possible. Unfortunately, I don't have an available spot for another six months. I will give you the contact information of colleagues you can reach out to.«

One of them was Dr. Ansgar Feil. Even though he also mentioned over the phone that he didn't have an available spot in the near future, he gave me an appointment for an initial consultation. It took place a week later and lasted fifty minutes, which is the usual length of a therapeutic consultation.

»Why do you think therapy would be the right or necessary measure for you?«

A good question, and as I was about to answer, the sentence popped out: »At the beginning of my dysacusis, I didn't even begin to think that I could be the problem.«

He looked deep into my eyes at this phrase.

»That you could be the problem?«

At the end of our conversation, he surprised me in an unexpected way.

»I offer to get in touch with colleagues and send you the addresses of three therapists by email, where you can start as soon as possible.«

I have never experienced a comparable level of support from conventional medicine. Amidst all the destructiveness, indifference, and insensitivity I had encountered and would continue to encounter, this was a completely different emotional level. I certainly had been lucky.

The CD never played again.

***

One topic of the conversation with Dr. Feil was the ›zero line‹ and how it shifts over time. Being on the ›zero line‹ means that you don't have much skill. Everyone above it is better, with a tendency towards the unattainable. Those below can do even less and are therefore not to be taken seriously.

Much of the music business runs on word of mouth. However, this does not necessarily have to happen within the scene. It can happen that doors open through completely different paths. Jens, to whom I already owed my kitchen job, had trained as a locksmith and was unemployed for a long time.

»Have you ever heard of the musical ›Cats‹? It's coming to Hamburg. I might get a job with a company that provides technical support for the musical.«

I remember it was a big event for the city when ›Cats‹ opened in April 1986. But I never thought about whether I would play there one day.

In April 1989, the phone rang: »Hello, this is Rainer. I'm the bass player for ›Cats‹. I got your number from Jens. He works here and told me that you're a great bass player. Would you like to play as a sub for me?«

Dude, of course I agreed and received the materials for the audition. An orchestra was put together with potential subs and the musical was played through in its entirety. This meant that the entire opus, which lasted two and a half hours, had to be perfectly prepared. Immediately afterwards, the conductor would announce who made the cut.

I practised for two weeks, eight hours a day. I remembered a significant phrase from Detlev, which he dropped years ago during a lesson: »You have to practise turning the pages.«

What a message! And since the bass part of some

pieces consisted of ten or more pages, I paid close attention to this.

The audition went perfectly. The conductor gave me the thumbs up, and I was able to play my first official performance the next day. Until 2001, over five hundred shows followed for me. On January 28, 2001, the last ›Cats‹-show in Hamburg took place.

Another aspect of professional music-making becomes clear here. In many genres, it doesn't matter whether you have an academic degree. I was never asked if I had studied. You go to an audition, play and either you are good enough or not.

But back to the ›zero line‹. When I came to Hamburg, it was at the level of a slightly advanced ambitious beginner and ›Cats‹ was out of reach. Four years later, ›Cats‹ was the ›zero line‹.

***

In mid-March 2017, I paid a visit to the audiometry department of an important Hamburg clinic. It had been recommended to me by several people for its professional diagnostic capabilities. The examinations, which took place in a kind of recording studio, were the most intensive I had experienced so far. They were carried out by a specially trained staff member.

I found the attempt to determine the intensity poor. He handed me a pair of headphones.

»Please let me know if the volume of the sound played through the headphones overpowers your tinnitus.«

Since my noises were made up of a complex, three-dimensional mixture, I always heard something from them, even when the sound being played was extremely loud.

»Now« I shouted to put an end to it all.

I was led into the consultation room and a doctor took a seat.

»What have you done so far?«

»I had the ITS done a few weeks ago.«

»That was far too late.«

He shook his head. A reaction that stayed with me the whole time. No matter which doctors I had seen or was yet to see, heads were often shaken to express disbelief regarding treatments carried out by colleagues.

»You have a significant dip at three kHz in your right ear. That could be the cause of your distortion. I recommend having a hearing aid made that emphasizes this area. The resulting linear progression may be able to neutralize your dysacusis.«

I found this suggestion adventurous and implausible. The part of my hearing that was already damaged was to be put under additional strain? This assessment was later confirmed by Robert Kroll, the alternative practitioner for laser therapy. I did not pursue this idea any further.

»I'll give you the brochure of a psychosomatic day clinic in Hamburg. The range of treatments includes tinnitus.«

I took it, but didn't feel any need for it yet. I found the following statement extraordinary: »Your problem is that you suffer from an illness that doesn't seem lucrative enough for scientific research. Therefore, from a conventional medical point of view, no effective treatment can be expected in the near future.«

So millions in our society suffer from tinnitus, and it's not lucrative for research? I don't have to understand everything. As the whole event felt extremely strange, I didn't ask any further questions. If he says it like that, it must be true.

The constant shrugging that haunted me did not spare me even here.

The Acupuncture

I wanted someone I could trust to tell me reliably what effects to expect from which therapy and the correct approach. Such a confidant didn't exist. My biggest fear was trying something that could make my tinnitus even worse. That wasn't easy.

All the conventional doctors I had consulted so far had their problems with alternative approaches. However, as no more ideas came from that side anymore, I started researching acupuncture and laser therapy.

It was easy with acupuncture. The internet is full of pages on the subject, but laser therapy was not. Most of the few I found were negative. There were hardly any testimonials, and this treatment was also relatively expensive.

I plucked up my courage and called Mr. Kroll. We made an appointment for a free consultation at his practice, which was four bus stops away. Was this quackery or the saviour?

At first, I tried to form an impression based on the outward appearance of the practice. Finally, I went to the entrance and pressed the button labelled *Private Practice*. A slim man opened the door, taller and younger than me. The sound of his voice was reassuring, a feeling I had already experienced during our phone call.

I knew from visiting his website that I was meeting someone who had suffered from tinnitus since the age of fifteen. Later, dysacusis and hyperacusis were added.

Mr. Kroll led me through the waiting area to his office. Apart from me, there was no other patient present. On the desk was a laptop and a portable device for hearing tests. It seemed more improvised than I was used to, but it had little to do with voodoo. I became more relaxed.

»I can take away the fear that your tinnitus will become chronic and never go away. Tinnitus doesn't settle in the cerebral cortex. It originates in the inner ear and stays in the inner ear. Regardless, I would still consider your condition highly acute.«

This sounded completely different to anything I had heard before.

»I have tried various therapies myself« he continued. »None of them helped, but I was able to live with it for a long time. When it became unbearable a few years ago, I went searching again. I came across laser therapy and started treatment. After two years, I only had a slight noise, and the other symptoms were gone. I then decided to offer laser therapy in my practice.«

In ENT practices, the hearing test generally goes up to eight kHz. This is completely sufficient to diagnose the need for a hearing aid. The range up to eight kHz is responsible for speech intelligibility. However, for the possible determination of tinnitus, it is definitely too limited as it is usually higher. Mr. Kroll carried out two hearing tests that went up to twelve kHz. One through the ears, as I was familiar with, and one through the skull bones. He then showed me the curves and was the first to explain in detail what was visible on them.

»The physical cause of your tinnitus and hearing distortion may lie in the dips. You can also clearly see that your air conduction and bone conduction diverge early on, especially in the right ear. I can imagine that you feel pressure on this ear.«

I actually did feel pressure at times.

The conversation lasted ninety minutes. I realized that it made a huge difference to talk to someone who knew from personal experience what you were talking about, and not just from reading about it. Nevertheless, I still couldn't bring myself to undergo treatment and initially decided in favour of acupuncture.

***

Over the years, an alarm function has developed in me regarding first impressions on people. This is mainly based on the sound and expression of the voice. The art lies in recognizing when to listen to it and when not to. As is often the case.

Through my work at ›Cats‹, I came into contact with a ›gala-band‹ in the spring of 1992. When I heard the voice of Peter, the musical director, over the phone, it immediately gave me an unpleasant feeling as it hit my eardrums. Since this engagement followed directly after my failed attempt to become a rock star, I was grateful for it.

The level of musicians in the gala scene is very high in some cases, and the events they play can be very exclusive. Such bands also serve as backing bands for artists, mostly from the pop music industry. One could call it upscale dance music.

Our stage outfit consisted of a glitter jacket combined with white pants and white shoes. That's why I still call them my ›Glitter-Jacket-Band‹ today. Peter attached great importance to performing everything live. Again, I had the advantage of being able to play the synth basses live, and I brought out the shoulder keyboard from the storeroom.

It was my first experience with a musical director in the classical sense. Peter was very skilled at picking out songs from CDs and writing arrangements for the band. Next to the telephone, the fax became the most important device in my flat. At times, multipage sheet music arrived here daily. I would then take these faxes to a copy shop to have them printed on proper paper.

As competent as Peter was in musical matters, he was incompetent when it came to people management; he was completely miscast in the position of a band leader. That happens more often. I had experienced it to some extent in my first Top-40 band as well, but never to such an extreme degree, and hopefully never again.

He made it a ritual to pick out one of the musicians at every rehearsal and at the sound check before the concerts, humiliating them in front of the whole team. You could get the impression that he enjoyed doing this.

Although there was a manager to whom officially the band belonged, Peter had the power to fire people, which he clearly enjoyed. He was able to pinpoint everyone's weak spots and exploit them perfectly. However, I was largely spared of this. After two years, I had a phone call with him where I expressed my thoughts on the matter. Surprisingly, he seemed affected by it and things improved temporarily.

The situation did not last long. After a few weeks, the humiliation started again. He just couldn't shed his skin. For me, that was the beginning of the end. After three years, I left and my ›Glitter-Jacket-Era‹ was history.

***

I attended a talk by a conversation therapist for tinnitus patients. I remember a former policeman who told that he always had an ear bud in one of his ears during special missions; he was convinced that this caused his tinnitus. Former, because he had to quit his job as a result. That sounded familiar to me.

What bothered me about the conversation was the message that there is no possibility of a cure. You could only try to find a way to deal with it in the best possible way. What a load of rubbish! That was definitely not my way. I asked her about acupuncture.

»Find a doctor who is familiar with traditional Chinese medicine, preferably one who comes from China. I don't recommend conventional doctors who offer acupuncture as an additional service.«

I searched and found Dr. Jin Sun. I contacted him by email and sent a completed questionnaire about my medical history. He then offered me an appointment two days later, which would also be free of charge.

Dr. Sun's practice, who also has a degree in conventional medicine, is located in HafenCity. I would describe the atmosphere as sober, not particularly different from the practices of conventional doctors I know. The team consisted of him and Mailin Chen, his assistant. She was a cheerful person who liked to talk and laugh, he was a calm and thoughtful man.

Dr. Sun took his time and answered my questions in great detail. This did not change during the entire treatment period and made him likeable and trustworthy despite his seriousness.

»It is not an advantage that you've had your tinnitus for so long«, he said with cautious optimism.

»You should avoid physical and mental stress two hours before and two hours after the acupuncture. Are you currently undergoing any other treatments? It is important that all other examinations are completed before we start.«

»I have the final meeting regarding the ITS in two weeks.«

»Let's wait for that before we start. Two weeks won't make a difference«

He expressly advised me to take Ginkgo, but recommended that I change the product I had been using.

»Not all Ginkgo products are the same.«

***

The Reeperbahn and its surroundings fascinated me from the very beginning. In contrast to today, in the eighties, it was a classic red-light district with countless table-dance clubs, peep shows and sex theatres with live fucking on stage. Ships had large crews, and lots of sailors roamed the streets hooting during shore leave, unmistakable in their uniforms. I often think that I arrived just in time to experience this flair, which is now largely gone.

I first came to the area for work in the mid-nineties. More precisely, to Große Freiheit, one of the main side streets of the Reeperbahn.

It's common for several bands to share a rehearsal room for cost reasons, coordinating when each can practise. During my Hard-Rock era, the drummer of another band approached me: »Would you like to sit in the box office at a sex theatre? A friend of mine is looking for someone for his club.«

I was torn about coming into contact with this scene so suddenly. Despite all my reservations, there were two arguments that persuaded me to accept: I could earn money during the week, which is not common for musicians. And I would never again have such an opportunity to peek behind the scenes of the red-light district.

There were several shows per shift. It started at eight in the evening and finished at four in the morning. When I was busy playing music, someone else would be there. In the first few weeks, I struggled to acclimate, which also manifested as sleep difficulties. The whole genre was far too foreign. On top of that, I immediately fell in love with one of the actresses and wanted to … let's call it … rescue her. I was pretty much on the fence, and it took me a while to realize that she didn't want to be rescued at all.

After the difficult early days, everything became more normal. I had daily contact with hookers, pimps and rockers. I learned a lot about the milieu, life and myself. Four years later, the engagement ended. The stories I experienced during that time buried the naive person from the Swabian province. I was thirty-five and had grown up in more ways than one.

Together with my earnings from music, it was an exceptionally lucrative period, perhaps the most profitable phase of my career so far. It laid the foundation for me to currently have no financial problems.

***

Three weeks after my last eardrum injection, I went for a follow-up appointment. Dr. Meinard performed a final hearing test and found that one of the dips in my left ear had improved.

»Is that due to the ITS or because I've been using my ear protection daily for six weeks and avoiding loud noises?«

»It's hard to say for sure, of course. Both will have contributed to this. It's possible that over the coming years, your brain will adjust to your hearing curve and the dysacusis will disappear.«

A few days later, I started acupuncture. Ten sessions over a period of four weeks. I paid in cash and after the registration process, Mrs. Chen led me into the waiting room. Here, I sat with a man whose partner was currently receiving her first treatment. We talked, and it turned out that he didn't think much of acupuncture. When she came in beaming and telling us how much it had helped her, he smiled dismissively. Mrs. Chen escorted me into the treatment room.

»Please undress to your underpants and t-shirt and lie down.«

She covered me with a linen sheet and left the room. Hundreds of thoughts ran through my mind. How could sticking needles into my body make the tinnitus disappear? Is what was going to happen going to hurt?

Dr. Sun came in shortly afterwards.

»How are you feeling?«

»Thank you, everything's fine so far.«

»Please sit up.«

I heard a crackling sound as he unwrapped the foil-wrapped needles. His fingers began to palpate my neck. Then I felt the brief pain that promised cure. I wondered how deep these needles would go into my flesh as the second prick was made.

»Please lay back down slowly again.«

You want me to lay down on the needles? I complied with his request and felt them. It was strange, but not unpleasant.

He inserted a total of sixteen needles, most of them mirrored, on the left and right side of my body – forearm, palm, calf, foot. Lastly, my head – forehead, temple, upper lip. My back, stomach, upper arms and thighs were never treated.

I hardly noticed most of the punctures. A few were associated with a slight pain. At one point on the palm of my left hand, however, it went through me like a bolt of lightning. Dr. Sun looked intensely into my eyes. He never acupunctured here again.

»Can you feel the needles? It's important that you feel the needles.«

After he left, I looked at the ceiling. What a freaky trip!

»All good?«

Ten minutes had passed, half-time.

»I have to flick the needles now so you can feel them again. That's very essential.«

Mrs. Chen was very pleasant in her dealings with the patients. The process was mostly relaxing. It was more uncomfortable with the needles that had caused pain during insertion. After another ten minutes, she removed them all, which was quick and uncomplicated.

Dr. Sun came again.

»Did you tolerate everything well?«

»I think so.«

»Good. You shouldn't do anything strenuous for the next two hours. Goodbye.«

I felt physically exhausted as I left the practice.

During the treatment period and the weeks that followed, my tones not only continued to wander, they began to become airy. Eventually, the high one barely existed, and the lower one was in the process of dissolving. The room-filling noise in my head continued to evolve, becoming louder at various points in different frequency ranges. The satisfaction that the intrusive noise was on the retreat far outweighed this development.

Was this a result of the ITS or the acupuncture? It doesn't matter. Only one thing was important for me: the tinnitus became quieter.

The Psychotherapy

It was the beginning of April and the three-month barrier had been broken. Dr. Feil sent me the promised email with the addresses. They were three female therapists. My first thought was that, in his opinion, I should deal with a woman. When I told this to my later therapist, she said that it was conceivable, but not essential. There are simply more females than males.

»You can have conversations with multiple therapists simultaneously on your health insurance card. Up to five each. Take advantage of this. It may take time to find someone you feel comfortable with.«

This had been explained to me by both the health insurance company and Dr. Feil. I immediately took care of arranging initial consultations and was able to organize them to take place within a week.

It was strange to tell the same stories over and over again. I tried to make sure I always did it with the same level of detail.

I have always found it difficult to convey decisions that involve rejections. In the music scene, a phone call was the common method for such procedures; face-to-face meetings were the exception. Leaving a message on an answering machine was considered bad form. In this case, all three of them thought I should do just that. Topsy-turvy world.

After the first conversation, I said goodbye to the youngest of the trio, who was just half my age. Maybe I'm doing her an injustice, but she seemed a bit awkward to me. This circumstance didn't work.

I used two criteria to help me make my final decision. Dr. Gudrun Herzfeld's practice was located slightly outside the city. To reach her from the S-Bahn station, I had to walk through Jenischpark. Here, I could sit on one of the benches, sort out my thoughts, and watch the dogs play on the large field. But more importantly, during our previous conversations, she had triggered reactions in me that I can best describe as a feeling of unease in my stomach. Her way of questioning evoked emotions.

***

Years ago, a colleague explained his selection criteria for joining a band to me as follows: »There are three components. You really like the music that is being played. The chemistry in the band is good. The pay is good. If two of these apply, you can go for it.«

He may have been right, though looking back now, I would prioritize the second point the most.

In the mid-nineties, a recommendation again led me to a Top-40 band. It was a company with an above-average booking situation.

The first meeting was about business matters. I had to invest a five-figure sum before the decimal point. The atmosphere in the room felt oppressive. The excellent earning potential, which meant that my investment would be recouped after a few months, made me ignore it. Unfortunately, this impression proved to be correct in the long term.

We played two, sometimes three times every weekend. The atmosphere in the backstage area could only be described as tense. It was clear that after years of working together, some members could barely stand to be in the same room. The whole thing was covered up with a lot of sarcasm and extensive alcohol and marijuana consumption. As known, I was not averse to this kind of leisure activity, having experienced cool gigs in a stoned state in the past. However, the quality of the performances suffered noticeably for the organizers and the audience, and it soon became clear that I was on a sinking ship. I went on stage in a drugged state and created my own realm by giving myself an incredible volume level via the monitor. In other words, it was extremely loud, without ear protection of course.

As if that wasn't enough, there were events that played their part in the whole dilemma. After just a few months, on the way to the gig, I wished I was already on my way home. Instead, one afternoon on the way to a tent festival, I passed a group of skinheads marching towards the festival site. Holy shit, I thought.

Usually the tent wasn't very full at the start of an event, but that changed within the first hour. That evening, there was no real atmosphere. The twenty bald guys were in the tent and partied in their own way in their combat boots, which was associated with jostling and other annoyances for those present. From the stage, I could see how the aggression in the room became more and more violent and resulted in many people leaving or not coming in at all.

When it became clear that it wouldn't be long before the tensions would escalate, a delegation of the organizers entered the tent, presumably farmers from the region. They went straight to the aggressors and did what they had to do. Within a very short time, the villains were lying on the ground and being carried out of the tent.

To be clear, the farmers remained standing and kicked them out and from those who were kicked out, there was no more sign. However, the tent only filled up moderately and the party remained subdued until the end. Perhaps the organizers should have kicked them out earlier.

All of this led to me losing the fun of making music more and more. After three years, I pulled the ripcord. I called the band leader. Here I learned that money is not the most important thing. And I would never agree to pay a large sum to join a band again.

***

Dr. Herzfeld radiated a pleasant femininity. Her voice was soft, and her way of dressing gave the impression that she also had at least some hippie spirit in her.

»There's behavioural therapy, psychotherapy and psychoanalysis. I could imagine the second option for you.«

- Firstly, the behavioural therapy:[*]

It differs from psychoanalysis in the following assumptions: It is assumed that behaviours can be learned and also unlearned. However, genetic differences are also taken into account as causes of disorders, for example in the so-called vulnerability-stress models. An inherited susceptibility to stress is considered as a precondition for a disorder. [...] It follows that problematic behaviour is primarily seen as the result of learning processes and should be changed through the use of behavioural and learning principles. A precise behavioural analysis is crucial in order to determine the current causes of the problematic behaviour. The treatment strategies are then individually adapted to the patient's problems. In order to bring about change, it is not necessarily necessary to determine the exact origins of the psychological issue. It is particularly effective for well-defined, less complex mental disorders.

---

[*] Source (as at 01.10.2023): https://de.wikipedia.org/wiki/Verhaltenstherapie
original language: german

- Secondly, the depth psychology-based psychotherapy:[*]

It is based on fundamental assumptions of depth psychology. The word ›depth‹ in depth psychology refers both to the hidden depth of the unconscious (unconscious or misunderstood desires, motives and conflicts) and to the ›depth of time‹, i.e. the continuing influences from childhood and adolescence. In the context of DP, it is assumed that deep-seated, unconscious psychological processes have an influence on a person's mental health. From this perspective, unconscious conflicts or repressed experiences are a sensible starting point for treating mental disorders. In contrast to behavioural therapy, the focus is therefore much less on directly influencing the patient's behaviour and more on clarifying the underlying causes, which should indirectly or subsequently lead to a reduction in symptoms.

- Thirdly, the psychoanalysis:[†]

The diagnostic psychoanalytically oriented conversation is designed as an unstructured, spontaneous interview. The focus is on the relationship aspect, less on the content aspect. The basis of the process is the therapist's friendly, waiting and non-directive attitude. The client's spontaneous behaviour provides information about his unconscious motivations and psychodynamic connections. Likewise, typical recurring patterns of behaviour in connection with the client's interpersonal contacts are revealed. The analyst's open attitude encourages the client to develop an initial readiness for transference. It is essential that the anamnesis of interests, strokes of fate and current life situation does not interrupt the dynamics of the initial interview.

[*] Source (as at 01.10.2023):
https://de.wikipedia.org/wiki/Tiefenpsychologisch_fundierte_Psychotherapie
original language: german

[†] Source (as at 01.10.2023):
https://de.wikipedia.org/wiki/Psychoanalyse#Das_diagnostische_Gespr%C3%83%A4ch
original language: german

As I understood it, behavioural therapy is about learning how best to deal with your situation. Psychotherapy lasts longer. You talk to each other once a week while sitting opposite each other. Psychoanalysis goes deeper. Here you meet more often per week and lie on the couch while the therapist sits behind you, moderating less.

»With psychotherapy, you still have to decide whether you want to do short-term or long-term therapy. Short-term therapy consists of twelve sessions with the option of a further twelve. Long-term therapy is sixty, which can be extended if necessary. Your decision is not final, you can also change later.«

I immediately knew that I wanted the longer trip. A week later, I communicated my decision.

»With the short one, I feel the pressure to have to get to the point as soon as possible.«

»I can understand that very well. The application will now go to a reviewer, who has five weeks to make a decision. It may happen that there's a time gap before the final approval by the health insurance company, and we have to take a break.«

In my case, there were no problems. With the remaining sessions still available on my health insurance card, it was a seamless transition.

When I walked through Jenischpark, I sometimes thought about what I wanted to talk about that day. I often found myself excluding topics because they seemed embarrassing or unpleasant. That's exactly why you have to talk about it, I thought. Easier thought than done.

From conversation to conversation, I became more confident, which made it easier. And so it wasn't long before I first heard the sentence that triggered my thought processes: »Do you recognize the pattern?«

But it was still a long way to the sentence »Have you noticed that today is the first time you didn't talk about your tinnitus?«.

The Relapse

It was beautiful spring weather in mid-April. I went out into the fresh air more and more often, and my general state of health improved.

During one of my walks along the Elbe, I ran into Tim. We didn't really know us, but it was enough to take note of each other and stop to talk. I told him about my current situation, and he mentioned his long-time friend Ramon Kramer, a songwriter from Hamburg. The next day, my phone rang.

»Hey, Werner. As you already know, I've spontaneously got two gigs lined up for the end of the month, and I'm still looking for a bass player. I sing and play guitar myself. Would you be up for it? We would perform as a trio with Tim on keyboards. There are no drums, so it won't be loud.«

That sounded like a good opportunity to find out whether it would be possible to make music again in such a setting – quietly, in the early evening, for one hour.

In consultation with Dr. Pielke, I agreed. It made sense to him that I needed to experiment independently of my sick leave to assess my situation.

During preparation, I played the MP3s so quietly on my laptop that the bass was just barely audible. We met twice to go through the songs. Then the concerts took place.

It was strange to play in front of an audience sitting on chairs and listening attentively. I had to concentrate hard to follow the subtle nuances of the program through my ear protection. You couldn't tell from the outside that I was very tense and preoccupied with myself. But I didn't have any problems afterwards and was encouraged in my hope that I would soon be able to professionally return to music.

***

My experiences with the singer-songwriter scene were limited. Around the turn of the millennium, I came into contact with a singer and actress named Sabine, who was without a permanent engagement at the time. My Top-40 era was behind me, and I was ready to new, especially creative projects. Together with two other musicians, we arranged a first rehearsal to get to know each other. I had got into the habit of recording events like this some time ago. This made post-processing much easier. With the help of such recordings, I have performed entire musicals without rehearsal when I have stepped in at short notice. Sometimes my colleagues gave me a weary smile as they thought I was exaggerating.

At this rehearsal, there were four dictaphones ready; I had to chuckle.

We started arranging Sabine's songs for our line-up, wanted to perform concerts and release a CD. Due to the experiences I've had over the years with relationships within bands, it's an unwritten rule for me to avoid such situations as much as possible. The stress for everyone involved is inevitable. I soon noticed signals from Sabine, but did not respond to them.

Over the months, an intensive working situation developed between her and me. As I had already set up a room in my flat as a recording studio, she came several times a week. We worked on the arrangements and created initial recordings.

It came as it had to come. However, the first phase, which was normally accompanied by butterflies, was nipped in the bud as she began to withdraw from one day to the next. Suddenly she didn't want all that anymore.

Furthermore, Sabine had made contact with a renowned producer, and I believed that he was not the right fit for her and the band.

That was the final straw and the relationship was over after less than a month. Without saying goodbye to me and the other band members, she left Hamburg a few weeks later to go to Munich, to work with him alone.

Five years later, I played there. I got in touch with her, and we met in a small café. On that occasion, she told me, among other things, that I had been right about everything concerning the producer. Who would have thought.

I've never seen her since.

***

Over the decades, it has become increasingly clear what price you have to pay for my lifestyle. It's difficult to establish and maintain a private environment. Just the fact that you're always on the road when others meet up or invite you to parties is a major obstacle. It's even difficult among musicians. You have contact with the colleagues you play with. When musical paths diverge, it often results in losing touch privately as well.

As I naturally aged slowly but surely, the audience in the clubs regularly renewed itself and became younger and younger in proportion. Most of the time I was on my own, occasionally I had a fling, but usually only for a short time. Due to the circumstances described above, the main opportunity of meeting women was to approach them during the concert breaks. Admittedly, that wasn't a big problem. But the tendency was more and more that these women could be my daughters.

I decided to explore a dating site. After a few months of little happening, I wanted to delete my account. That's when I saw a new profile with the following text:

›I'm looking for a long-haired musician with a house by the lake and a motorcycle in the garage.‹

Well, that sounded good!

From my side, I brought up a bald musician with a rented flat in Hamburg-Altona and a motorcycle on the centre strip. Since then, Petra and I have been a couple and have what is called a long-distance relationship.

When it suited us, we went to concerts, frequently to see the heroes of our youth. On May 2, another such event was coming up – IRON MAIDEN at the Hamburg ›Barclaycard Arena‹. We had bought the tickets long before I started having problems with my ears. Over the past few months, I've often pondered whether I should go or stay at home. In hindsight, many people know everything better, including myself. However, I have the impression that the upcoming incidents are not as easy to explain as they first seem.

At the beginning of May, I was in a good mood. The psychotherapy was requested, a rejection was unlikely, and the concerts with Ramon had been successful. The remaining sound was only sporadic and the noise was so quiet that I was able to sleep largely relaxed again after many weeks. At that point, I realized what an important factor this is for quality of life. As long as I could sleep reasonably well at night, I was able to get through the day with the tinnitus. The nights I spent tossing and turning were the most exhausting of the past months. I should mention at this point that my distortion hasn't changed, but the hypersensitivity has improved significantly.

Our seats were located at the back of the first tier, far away from the stage. We had sat here a few years ago at a MOTÖRHEAD-concert and were amused by the tough bikers who clearly felt comfortable in the plush armchairs. Back then, we felt rather out of place. It just didn't fit with a heavy metal concert. Now I was happy to be sitting here.

For my ears, I decided on double protection. I had inserted the 25-dB filters and brought my construction site earmuffs with me, which I planned to put on top if needed. I felt well-prepared.

After just a few minutes, I could feel it all over my body. It wasn't so much about the volume, but the pressure and the vibrations, created by the deep bass. I probably should have just stood up and left. But I stayed and as a result, I was stressed throughout the entire concert.

›Hopefully this turns out okay!‹ Already on the way home, I had a feeling that it wasn't going to be.

The next morning, this feeling had become a reality. A sharp, aggressive sound had settled in the left area of my head. The old one, on the other hand, had completely disappeared, or to put it another way: my tinnitus had become very loud again overnight, but it was completely different from before.

***

I didn't really like big halls like that, and I never liked festivals because of the crowds. Sometimes it just couldn't be avoided. The last concert of this size that Petra and I went to was a year and a half ago.

In my youth, there were two bands or artists that influenced me. First DEEP PURPLE, later FRANK ZAPPA. I never saw DEEP PURPLE live. That was because I was too young, and such bands didn't play in the direct vicinity of my hometown. I experienced FRANK ZAPPA several times, but unfortunately not in what I considered to be his best and most creative period in the early to mid-seventies, for the same reasons. In Hamburg, MILES DAVIS joined the mix.

Both FRANK ZAPPA and MILES DAVIS enjoy great recognition in my professional environment. It's a different story with the woman who entered my musical life during my time in Spaldingstraße. MADONNA captivated me from the very beginning. Whenever I mentioned this in a conversation with colleagues, a certain irritation would spread. I have to admit that I flirted with it.

There are many musicians who impress me from a technical point of view, even fascinate me, but don't trigger anything. And then there are those who evoke emotions in me, take me on a journey, transport me to another world – regardless of their technical ability.

›Madge‹ clearly belongs to the second category. But I've never thought about going to one of her concerts.

I was just sitting on the sofa at Petra's when I found a clue while surfing the Internet.

»Hey, sweetie, I've just seen that MADONNA is performing in Cologne. Do you want to go with me?« Meant more as a joke, cue IRON MAIDEN.

I was surprised by the answer: »I'm not really interested in her, but I'm down for a few days in Cologne.«

Crazy.

I got the tickets. We booked a flat and a few months later, we travelled to the Rhine for five days. Since I knew people there, it was an entertaining time. A nice mixture of strolling around the city, visiting friends and the indescribable pleasure of a show by this artist. It was November 5, 2015 and the last concert I was able to enjoy without a care in the world.

***

In my renewed fear and despair, I first contacted Dr. Sun. He got back to me quickly and gave me an appointment for the next day.

»You underestimated the situation,« he said, looking me in the eyes with a serious expression. The reproach in his words was unmistakable.

»I offer you a treatment of five sessions. After that,

however, a break of at least two months must be maintained.«

I had thought I was as good as cured, but the incidents of the last few days had set me back months. Had it become permanent and chronic after all? It could no longer be avoided.

I had to wrap up everything that was on hold. The band, which had been my main source of income in recent years, needed a concrete statement, as my sub understandably had to plan. I passed on the job of mixing a CD to a colleague. I had now completely disappeared from the scene. If at all, I would have to start more or less from scratch after all this shit.

About Side Effects and the Medical Service

Shortly after the end of the first acupuncture cycle in March, I experienced a strong reaction from my body. There was a spot on the inside of my left forearm that I always felt distinctly during needling. The result was an unpleasant tingling sensation in the palm of my left hand. One evening, this developed into a numbness that affected the entire left side of my body. As the symptoms did not improve by the next morning and were even more pronounced, I began to search for possible causes and found stroke and heart attack. I didn't think it was one of the two, but I wanted to play it safe. Especially as the time factor also plays a major role here.

It was a Sunday morning when I went to the emergency room at the University Hospital Eppendorf. After a five-hour wait, I was picked up by a doctor. He carried out several tests, couldn't find anything conspicuous and discharged me home as healthy. My symptoms largely disappeared over the course of the day, and a few weeks later the tingling was gone.

Now, after the second acupuncture cycle, I felt the tingling again. As for the tinnitus, it became more relaxed and quieter for a day after each session. Then it returned to its original level.

A big advantage of the new situation was that I could spare myself the destructiveness I experienced at the beginning of my illness. I now directly contacted the doctors with whom I had had positive experiences. From a conventional medical point of view, this was Dr. Meinard. I went to see him the second time in mid-May. Since I was prompt in seeking help this time, we decided to proceed with the ITS once more.

After a few days, a siren formed behind my right ear, similar to that of an ambulance driving just a few meters behind you. I noticed that there are two different sirens for this type of vehicle. I had both of them, alternating around the clock. My sounds were one hundred percent identical to the originals.

I can't say whether this was a result of the injections. What I do know for sure is the pressure in my ear that developed immediately after the third session, where my right eardrum was punctured.

When I went to the car, the opposite ear was completely blocked from one moment to the next. I definitely couldn't hear anything anymore. After a few hours, my hearing slowly returned. From then on, however, I constantly felt this pressure sensation in both ears, as I knew it from taking off and landing in an airplane. At the same time, I also felt an unpleasant, low rumble when noise such as trucks in traffic were audible in everyday life.

»I don't think this is a side effect of the ITS. It is most likely a delayed hearing loss. The current treatment is exactly the right measure for this.« Dr. Meinard seemed certain.

After the last injection, I asked him how he would assess my professional situation.

»You can play the guitar quietly on the sofa, but under no circumstances should you plug it into a radio. It's still far too early for that. A few days ago, the ›medical service‹* approached me. I transmitted them the hearing curve from our last test.«

---

* The Medical Service (MD) is the socio-medical and nursing care advisory and assessment service of the statutory health and long-term care insurance.
The MD performs important tasks in the assessment of the need for long-term care and in quality assurance.
Source (as at 16.04.2024): https://www.bundesgesundheitsministerium.de/service/begriffe-von-a-z/m/medizinischer-dienst
original language: german

I had no idea what meaning this statement would soon have for me, I was initially amused by the phrase ›connect to the radio‹.

The treatment ended on May 30, one month after my relapse. Now I was supposed to take ›Trental 400 mg‹ again. I now knew that other sufferers had also experienced a sharp increase in their ringing in the ears as a result of taking this medication, but that it had helped. If it could make my tinnitus quieter, it was worth three weeks of madness to me.

I started with one pill a day, increased to two and finally to the recommended three. Undoubtedly, there was a clearly noticeable response again, but nowhere near as strong.

Basically, it should be noted that the second ITS did not have the same effect as the first. The sharp sound did not start to move, but remained where it was. My hypersensitivity to sound did not increase. The ambulance would follow me for months, and the massive pressure in my ear often haunted me.

I was plagued by various fears about the future, but I was much more stable than at the beginning of the year. I wasn't worried about what preparations I needed to make to avoid having to stay on this planet any longer than necessary. Above all, the fear of becoming chronic no longer played a role. For one thing, I was already in my fifth month anyway, and for another, I believed less and less in this spectre. In addition, the psychotherapy had been approved in the meantime, and the bleakness of January had given way to the friendliness of spring.

I got a call from a bandleader who was looking for a sub for his bass player. »I also had tinnitus once, but I didn't do anything about it at the time, and after six months it was gone again. To fall asleep, I always imagined a sailing boat going out to sea and taking the tinnitus with it.«

I changed that for myself to a hot air balloon with a small hole in it. The sounds that filled my head escaped slowly but steadily through the opening. At the same time, it flew up into the sky, became smaller, and the tinnitus became quieter.

There was a period of several weeks when I always woke up at four o'clock. It was as regular as clockwork. My noise was then extremely sharp and loud. After fifteen minutes it calmed down, became softer, and I continued to sleep. But there were still nights when nothing worked. What the heck, I'll just get up. I'll be ready to sleep again in a day or two. Then my body will be so tired that I won't be able to do anything against it.

It's amazing what you can get used to.

***

St. Pauli has a unique scene. Many clubs offer live music. Admission is free and the bands receive a fixed fee. As a musician, you have no financial risk in the form of taking at the door. As chance would have it, my career took me back to the Kiez.

In a café in Eimsbüttel, I met Otto, a fellow musician from my early days in Hamburg. He told me about a well-known club on the Reeperbahn that was in the process of setting up a house band and was looking for musicians. I applied and became a member of the CASH BOYS. I played countless gigs with Offel, the guitarist and singer, and Jan, the drummer, until 2015. Since then, I have known that nothing can replace blind understanding in a band.

The ›Lehmitz‹ was a pub with cult status – open 24 hours a day and seven days a week since the fifties. The toilets had no seats, beer was only served in bottles, and the place was cleaned out once at four in the morning.

In the beginning, we only played on Wednesdays, but over the years other days were added. People loved it, and after a short time the Lehmitz was always packed when the house band played. We had wireless systems for our instruments, played on the counter and in between. We were handed joints and gave them back after use, only to get the next one two meters away. Tequila flowed down our throats to warm us up, and the beers quenched our thirst.

Our stage was a small corner opposite the entrance. You had to pass by it to get to the toilets in the basement. During one of my first gigs, there was a scuffle in the entrance area, which was quickly put to an end by the bouncer and some guests. They joined forces to throw the troublemakers out onto the street. We played BILLY IDOL's *Rebel Yell* and rocked on throughout the entire situation.

After the gig, Joseph, the boss of it all, came up to me: »I was glad to see that you weren't phased by the incident.« He grinned over the entire width of his face.

»Oh, you know, I've experienced enough in the past few decades. I'm not that easily rattled anymore.«

»Scuffles like that happen from time to time, but our audience here is the stronger one when it comes to the crunch.« We laughed the way you laugh when you're in full control of a situation.

***

Although quite a few people around me had tattoos at the time, I wasn't interested in them for a long time. At the tender age of forty-five, that changed. I went to ›Jungbluth‹ in Marktstraße. One of the most traditional studios in Hamburg, where I knew the average waiting time was six months. I had never seen the inside of one before and wanted to take the opportunity to find out about the prices.

Several black-clad individuals with metal in their faces surrounded me as I climbed the two steps and stood in the small room, the walls of which were decorated with pictures of living works of art. A warm feeling washed over me and a pleasant nervousness accompanied me to the counter, above which a sign was displayed:

Piercing & Tattoo are addictive, best not to start.

I told them about my ideas.

»Alright, just have a seat for a moment, the right tattoo artist is taking a break and will come and see you.«

It was a beautiful, sunny day and I took a seat on a chair by the street. Serge arrived a little later. He was young, tall, broad-shouldered and, as befits his profession, tattooed all over. After a brief small talk, we discussed my project.

»Okay, that would take four sessions.«

»Cool, then I can go inside and ask when the next available appointment is.«

»A client cancelled tomorrow, if you want, you can take that slot.« Wow, there I was, having to make another one of those five-minute decisions.

For the following appointments, I was called if someone cancelled at short notice again; I got my tattoo amazingly quickly. The sign was right. I was already thinking about what I wanted to immortalize on my skin next, and soon there were more.

***

In principle, I have long belonged to the group that sees tinnitus primarily as a symptom of overuse of the inner ear. While the body used to only need a day to recover after going to the disco, it is no longer able to do so. However, I was sure that stress and a weakened psyche were factors that played a role. After all, not everyone with an overloaded inner ear ends up with a permanent tinnitus.

It was the beginning of June and I felt an increasing need to test my body. A smaller tattoo, doable in one session, seemed appropriate to me.

In the old town of Altona, there are still a few longstanding corner pubs that contribute significantly to the atmosphere. A few hundred meters from my flat, one of these pubs had been empty for months. At the beginning of the year, a tattoo studio moved in, whose staff regularly sat in front of it. I came to the conclusion that it was not fully booked and there was no need to worry about waiting for months. I made my way there, discussed everything with the owner, and showed up a week later for my appointment, which was supposed to last two hours.

The possibility that my relapse was not solely due to the volume, but also to the stress that my body and I had to deal with, was present. So there were several reasons to be nervous. Firstly, because of the blood-thinning Trental I was taking. Then because of the constant noise created by the machine and the permanent background music and, last but not least, because of the procedure itself. I closed my eyes, felt almost no pain, and there was hardly any bleeding.

At home, I wanted to make myself comfortable on the sofa, relaxing for the rest of the day. Just before six o'clock, the phone rang. I recognized the number of my health insurance company on the display.

»We've received a message from the ›medical service‹. After consultation with your ENT doctor, you have been determined to be fit for work with immediate effect.«

So much for relaxing. Quite apart from the fact that I was completely unprepared for the news, at that time it wasn't possible for me to ask Dr. Meinard how that could happen. Just a few days earlier, he had told me something completely different.

The next day began with a phone call to him: »There has been no further contact with the MD since the already mentioned inquiry.«

I went to see Dr. Pielke again without an appointment.

»I've never seen the ›medical service‹ simply cancel a doctor's sick note that has been valid for more than a week. I haven't been contacted yet. We now have to wait until the decision is in writing. A phone call alone is not enough for us to react in any way.«

There it was again, the snake. Why the hell wasn't I allowed to feel any joy? What power has anything against me? That has to change again at some point.

Finally, the letter was in my mailbox, with the following excerpt …

End of your incapacity for work
Dear Mr. Kolb,
The Medical Service of the Health Insurance Funds (MD)
supports insured persons, doctors, and health insurance companies with medical matters.
In consultation with your attending physician, the doctor advising the MD in North has come to the conclusion that your incapacity for work will end on June 9, 2017 and that you can therefore resume work from June 10, 2017.
Your attending physician has already been informed accordingly.

It should be noted that my attending physician is mentioned twice. The first time referring to Dr. Meinard, the second time to Dr. Pielke. His statement: »In the meantime, the MD has written to me. I advise you to submit a written objection and bring it to your office in person to have it acknowledged. This is not about you personally, they just don't want to pay.«

Pay? Here's a bit about payments: I have been paying

my contributions every month without interruption since 1992, have never been on sick leave in the past twenty-seven years, and have incurred minimal costs except for the usual examinations.

I have paid for all treatments such as osteopathy, ITS, acupuncture as well as pharmaceutical products such as Ginkgo, Trental and the serum for ITS myself, which amounted to over three thousand euros.

And now, after not receiving even a thousand euros in sick pay, I have been arbitrarily deemed fit to work again?

I asked Dr. Meinard for a statement, which he provided to me promptly. Together with my objection, I handed it in at the reception desk and received a receipt.

I felt more powerless than ever before. Were these the much-described slow turning wheels of bureaucracy? So far, my experience with government offices had been limited to the car registration office and the residents' registration office.

***

Basically, I don't believe in higher powers, predestination or providence. There were a few moments when I pondered for a second. If there really is such a thing, two of them would have neutralized each other in the following incident.

In 2002, I got a call from Willy. A sound technician who had crossed my path time and again over the years.

»Hello, Werner. Listen, I recently worked with Klaus Debusmann, a pianist. He often travels on cruise ships under his artist pseudonym MISTER RED SHOES and is looking for a bass player. Would you like me to pass on your number?«

He was supposed to, and it didn't take long for Klaus to get in touch with me. A few days later, we met at Hamburg Central Station. He was on his way to a ship, and we had an hour to get to know each other. Klaus was broad-shouldered, a head taller, and slightly older than me. Truly an impressive figure and, as I would soon discover, a devil at the keys with incredible energy. It looked like he spent most of the year sailing the world's oceans, which appealed to me immensely. But it also raised concerns.

Compared to my red light experiences, I probably wouldn't get a second opportunity like this. But I didn't want to be on the road so much or for so long. On the one hand, I saw the risk of jeopardizing my musical existence in Hamburg, and on the other, I was in a relationship with Stella. After a lot of back and forth, I agreed, especially as Stella didn't want me to miss out on this opportunity for her sake.

The bureaucracy involved was manageable. Applying for the necessary documents went off without a hitch. Some of it was organized by the shipping company.

My first trip took me through the Black Sea. Then five days at home, followed by two weeks on the east coast of the United States. I quickly realized that being on the road so much was exhausting. Additionally, I discovered that I was not immune of seasickness.

Next up was a trip to New Zealand. I bumped into Klaus at the airport. As we were sorting out the formalities at the counter, he had all our luggage checked in under his name. We had never done it that way before. Our flight took us via Frankfurt to Singapore. We had an overnight stay here before continuing on to Auckland. Once all the checks had been completed, we made ourselves comfortable in the gate area.

»So, have you got your passport with you?«

What was meant as a purely rhetorical question by Klaus made my cup of coffee slip out of my hand. It was in the drawer in my study, where it's always kept when I don't need it – providence number one.

What followed could be described as a certain amount of excitement and hustle and bustle. I called Stella.

»Hey darling, I need you to bring me my passport as soon as possible.«

»Where is it?«

Her route went from Barmbek to Altona, stopover, then Fuhlsbüttel. That took some time. I'll ignore the fact that I always left her the car for my absences as a possible intuition at this point.

The plan was to fly to Frankfurt one plane later. However, all the people behind their counters said that I would not make the connecting flight to Singapore. The time frame for this was thirty minutes and would be far too tight. The prerequisite for this undertaking to be conceivable at all was my luggage checked in on Klaus. This way, it remained on the plane and took off as scheduled – providence number two.

Stella arrived with the all-important document and my journey began. At that time I always took the bass as hand luggage, which was never a problem with Lufthansa. It was taken from me at the entrance and stored in a cupboard. After our arrival, it felt like an eternity until the passengers in front of me reached the exit, and I could receive my instrument from the stewardess and run off.

I had to cover a long distance to get from the arrivals to the departures. I kept on running and reached my gate at literally the last moment. The passengers had already boarded. Only Klaus was still standing there, along with the ship's officials. There you go.

When we were in Singapore, I got an impression of what it means to be successful worldwide. We were walking along a shopping street near our hotel. Music videos were playing on one of the large billboards attached to the building facades, and I saw artists whose videos I had watched at the airport in Hamburg a few hours earlier – impressive.

There was an extreme swell in the Tasman Sea. It was one of those moments when I spent most of my time hanging over the big white telephone. To make matters worse, one of our concerts was scheduled for that evening, and I dragged myself straight from the bathroom to the lounge.

It was going to be very special.

Due to the circumstances, there was hardly anyone in the hall, and I was more concerned with preventing my equipment from tipping over than actually playing music with it. However, I no longer felt any nausea. MISTER RED SHOES wasn't fazed by anything, and the few people present loved our performance.

That night, I woke up to a loud thud and the ship's loudspeakers played: »Captain to the Bridge, captain to the Bridge.«

The ship, which was relatively small for a cruise ship, stopped moving and became a plaything of the waves. The cupboard doors burst open and pieces of furniture flew through the cabin. In places, I could see water right in front of my porthole – Titanic live. For the next few hours, it was forbidden to leave the cabin. We were brought food and drinks until the announcement sounded: »Dear guests, we have succeeded in getting one of the engines going again. We are now heading for the nearest port.«

It was a crawl. Twenty-four hours later, we reached our destination, Lyttelton near Christchurch.

The ›Welt‹ reported at the time, December 16, 2002:*

House-high wave damages luxury liner ›Hanseatic‹-bridge window smashed in storm off New Zealand. Engine down. 87 passengers and 112 crew members of the luxury liner ›Hanseatic‹ escaped with a scare:

---

*Source (as at 01.10.2023):
www.welt.de/print-welt/article302715/Haushohe-Welle-beschaedigt-Luxusliner-Hanseatic.html
original language: german

The five-star ship of Hamburg-based Hapag-Lloyd Kreuz-fahrten GmbH was damaged in heavy weather east of New Zealand on Saturday morning. A wave about ten meters high smashed a bridge window. The ingress of water first paralysed sensitive electronics and ultimately also the main engine. As a result, the ›Hanseatic‹ drifted helplessly in the choppy sea. But only ›for a short time‹, spokeswoman Antje Borstel told the newspaper ›Welt‹ on Sunday, without, however, being able to narrow down the exact time period. The ship sustained material damage. Here, too, nothing could be said about the amount and extent of the damage.

In any case, there were no personal injuries. The ship's management under the command of Captain Thilo Natke always had the situation under control. According to Hapag-Lloyd, there was no danger to passengers or crew at any time. The ›Hanseatic‹, which entered service in 1993, came from the USA. The trip from Anchorage Bay should have ended in Dunedin (New Zealand). After the incident, the ship headed for the east coast port of Lyttelton further north. According to Borstel, the luxury liner has now arrived here. The passengers will be transported home from there.

I myself never had the feeling that the situation was life-threatening. But there were fellow travellers who experienced it differently.

The Laser Therapy

The idea that I could be forced by the MD's decision to resume my activity as a professional musician, with the associated stress for my ears, made me aggressive. My thoughts included the possibility that it was not in the interest of the healthcare system to heal, but rather to simply manage in order to maintain sources of income.

I was lucky that I didn't have to rely on sick pay. Building up reserves in good times is the key word here.

I grew up with the idea of saving for rainy days. It was customary at local parties to set up a private stach of beer as one of the first measures. Everyone would casually grab a bottle or two from the drinks supply and stash them in a secret place. The hard times were not long in coming. When the official stock ran out, the moment of truth arrived. You could score points by letting slip in a conversation that you knew a place that promised bliss. But there was also looting. Good for those who had a good nose here in more ways than one.

In the mid-nineties, I followed my instincts, jumped on the stock market train, and put a handful of this hippie-led company with the bitten fruit as a logo in my depot.

»Dude, are you crazy, they'll be bankrupt next year.« Those were the days.

***

In spring 2017, Daniel moved to Cologne for job reasons. On July 1, he hosted a house-warming party and sent me an invitation. I embarked on the journey with mixed feelings. A cold buffet, BBQ, around sixty guests, and a DJ promised a lavish party. The break eight weeks earlier had made me extremely insecure about anything related to loud noises. I had also only stopped taking Trental two days earlier.

I was able to stay with MICHI KLEIBER, whom I had met again after almost thirty years at the MADONNA concert in 2015. He was the singer in my very first band in Hamburg. In addition to his flat, he also has a room that serves as a production facility for his artistic activities. He had offered me the chance to stay here during future visits.

Since the relapse, I've had to deal with increasing level fluctuations. During the train ride, the orchestra in my head got louder from minute to minute, heralding a so-called ›crescendo‹ consisting of very different sound material. During the course of our first evening together, this culminated in a constant ›tutti‹, meaning that everyone was playing as loud as they could.

I still performed the ritual of drinking tea and taking valerian before going to sleep, as well as my trips in the hot air balloon. I had also got used to a special sleeping position. I lay down on my left side with my legs bent and – very importantly! – the blanket between them. This was definitely the only position that worked for me to fall asleep. However, at the moment, the success of these routines was limited. I stared into the darkness more often and didn't feel like I was getting any deep sleep.

After spending two nights like this, the day of the party had arrived. My plan was to take the period of development with me and be safe again before the big bang. When I arrived at around three o'clock in the afternoon, people were already busy preparing the cold buffet.

The exciting question at such events is whether you have anything to say to each other. More and more old friends from my youth arrived. I wasn't aware that they had all kept in touch over the decades. I chatted animatedly, but also noticed that the volume increased with each additional person in the room, making me feel more uncomfortable. Don't make a mistake now!

When the DJ set up his system at around seven o'clock, I started my farewell round and left the party a few minutes later. It was a shame to have to leave so early. But, from how I felt, I knew I had made the right decision.

The S-Bahn train departed, and I recalled the first time I had met MICHI KLEIBER.

***

During my preparations for moving in January 1985, Ebbe placed an advertisement for me. The February issue of the city magazine was already out at the kiosks days before my arrival, and Michi was the first to respond to it. Right after it was published, our shared phone rang: »When will he arrive in Hamburg?«

It was CITY NORD, an established band that was undergoing radical change. Michi had founded it several years ago with his childhood friend Frank and had already released two records with them. The way they both wore their hair, my parents' generation would have called them ›long-haired dachshunds‹ in the seventies. With a new bass player and second guitarist, CITY NORD was to be continued, and I got the job.

Dude, I'm going crazy!

We rehearsed in one of the typical bunkers, of which there are several in Hamburg. Our guitarist, the fourth member of the group, usually picked me up by car, while Michi took the S-Bahn. Frank, on the other hand, travelled by taxi and often brought electrical equipment to be tested. I had no idea about all this technical stuff and stayed out of it. It was evident that everything required money, and I had barely enough to survive. I frequently found myself being invited for a cup of coffee, which we consistently enjoyed during breaks at a nearby snack bar.

Right from the start, there was friction in terms of musical style and lyrics. Michi and Frank were no longer on the same page, which was probably normal after many years of previous history. As a result, the band broke up after a year and three concerts. Michi and I started another project with two jazz musicians and played together for a while before losing touch.

For the sake of completeness, there is one incident from our time with Frank. One evening after a rehearsal, we played pool together.

»Tell me, where did you get the money for all this equipment?«

He looked at me with wide eyes and seemed genuinely surprised by the question. He just said his last name, which of course I knew: »Otto?«

That was also one of the moments when I realized how naive I was often and still am. At that moment he uttered that one word, I understood that I had been playing music with one of the wealthiest people in this country the whole time.

***

For months, my thoughts had been centred on low level laser therapy. On the way back, as I reviewed the weekend and the associated soundscape, I remembered the words of Robert Kroll: »Tinnitus originates in the inner ear and remains in the inner ear. The laser supplies new energy, allowing it to regenerate even years later.«

While I was still on the train ride, I decided to tackle it now. Only then could I find out what was behind it and find peace regarding the matter.

A few days later, the tinnitus became quieter again. Was this because the Trental had left my body, the stress of travelling was over, or because I had made this decision? Either way, my choice was not influenced by this.

This journey into the unknown, which I of course paid for entirely myself, was to extend over ten stages. It was July 10, when I set off to the practice of Mr. Kroll for the second time.

First, he documented the current course of my hearing curve. Then it started, thirty minutes per ear. He switched on the device, adjusted the laser, and left the room. I felt a pleasant warmth in my ear canal and closed my eyes. It was striking how the creaking of the door at the other end of the room soon sounded as if it were being opened right next to my head.

»Everything's all right?«

»Everything's great.«

When I left the practice, my tinnitus was significantly more present.

The following day, the pressure on my ears was very pronounced. Mr. Kroll then changed the type of radiation at the second session. It was a Friday, and I drove to Petra's afterwards. As I glided along the highway, I noticed that the right side of my face felt more and more inflamed. Additionally, my hypersensitivity was developing more strongly than ever. Although I was sitting on the sofa in the living room, the clattering from the kitchen was almost unbearable. It was as if a whip was cracking in my right ear just by putting a plate on the kitchen table. In the course of Sunday, the cat o'nine tails was hung on the hook again.

Weeks ago, Dr. Pielke had suggested that I finally give my body and mind some rest. This weekend, I had the feeling that he might be right. I decided not to pursue anything new after the laser therapy.

***

At the ›Lehmitz‹, a change in leadership had taken place, which brought about some special modifications. Also in the house band policy. We took this as an opportunity to move to Hans-Albers-Platz with the CASH BOYS.

There were multiple clubs in this area that were supplied with bands by the same agency. Once you were part of this family, you could play every weekend and the fees were better.

There was a ritual of meeting up with other musicians in one of the clubs before the start of the evening. We would have a drink together, chat, and wish each other a successful weekend.

It was during one of these occasions that Henrik, a guitarist and singer, and I started philosophizing. How wonderful it would be to have a musical island. To simply be creative without any commercial pressures. The more we talked about it, the more appealing it became, and we decided to look for a drummer and make it happen.

The concept was to simply jam and record the sessions. Afterwards, we would review the ideas and decide which ones to develop further. It was really fun to turn these sessions into songs. As we often had to take breaks of several weeks, years went by before a concert programme was created and the time was ripe to present the result to the public. I started contacting clubs and was soon able to organize our first gig. The venue was pleasantly filled, and the reaction to our performance was surprisingly positive. It was not easy stuff that we played.

As I am convinced that there is an audience for every kind of music, I had enough motivation to get the band rolling. Then something strange happened. After this concert, Henrik could no longer be reached. He didn't answer the phone and didn't respond to any messages I left on his voicemail or emails for weeks. I've known musicians to back out of projects for various reasons as they became more concrete. But I never had experienced it like this before.

Months later, he finally got in touch and explained that

he had felt uncomfortable at the gig because he was the centre of attention. There is simply a difference between performing cover songs in some pub and presenting original material. In my opinion, he should have realized this sooner.

I wouldn't say that years of work were wasted. There were many wonderful moments and the original idea of creating a musical island was fulfilled. However, I left this experience with the thought that it may have been the last time I initiated a creative project of my own.

***

July 13, 2017. Call from the health insurance company. »You will receive a letter in the next few days. It contains a questionnaire about your workplace, which you must complete and return. The MD needs this information in order to make a decision in your case.«

When I held the questionnaire in my hands, I was once again stunned. A standard form with questions about a workplace, like you might find in a factory. They still hadn't understood that I earned my money as a freelance musician and not as an employee of a company. Just a few weeks ago, I had submitted Dr. Meinard's statement in which he expressed this unequivocally.

»That's completely normal«, Dr. Pielke explained to me. »From the authorities' point of view, you're just a case with a case number. It is not intended to familiarize yourself more deeply than necessary with such a case.«

So this was a common bureaucratic mechanism that totally ignored reality. While it may not be dramatic in other areas, I found it absolutely unacceptable and counterproductive to the actual purpose in my case. Instead of receiving support, the pressure was increased exponentially without any consideration of the facts. I included my own job description with this form:

My work as a freelance bassist primarily takes place at weekends. I usually leave my home between 3 and 6 pm, depending on how far I have to travel and the amount of work involved.

First, I load up the car with the necessary equipment. Then I drive to the location. This includes venues in Hamburg, tent festivals, shooting festivals, city festivals throughout northern Germany and the Ruhr area, as well as private events such as weddings, birthday parties, anniversaries, etc. Furthermore, engagements on cruise ships, which last 2–6 weeks.

After arrival at the venue, the backline is set up: Drums, guitar/bass amplifier and other instruments.

Depending on the event, there is normal pub/disco operation during this work. This means that there is loud music playing from a CD or another band is performing.

This is followed by the sound-check. Here, all instruments and vocal microphones are levelled, which is done at normal playing volume. The same applies to the monitor sound. This is used to check the individual musicians and the entire band.

There are two variants: With speakers placed in front of the respective musician, radiating towards them. Then, depending on personal requirements, the individual instruments are balanced in relation to the signals coming directly from the stage. This means, for example, that the singer's vocal signal must be loud enough here to be able to assert itself against drums, guitars, wind instruments, etc. What has to be put on this monitor and at what volume depends on the size of the stage in question.

The alternative to loudspeakers is in-ear monitoring. Headphones that are adapted to the ear canal. The principle of levelling is similar to that of loudspeakers.

When the sound-check is over, it may take several hours before the band starts. It rarely starts straight away. It depends on the venue whether there is a backstage-room where you can retire until the concert starts or whether you stay in the venue.

The playing time usually ranges between 8 pm and 3 am. During the breaks and during the dismantling, a DJ typically plays music.

Afterwards, I drive back home; if the gig is further away, a hotel is provided. Once home, the car is unloaded.

In good months, I have around 10–15 of these events. During the week, I prepare by learning new songs, acquiring new clients, or practising on my instrument.

My work as a freelance sound engineer is less pronounced in comparison, as I only completed my training for this 2 years ago.

For recording instruments and vocals, it is crucial to place the microphones correctly to ensure clean and perfect signals. This requires maximum concentration and can take several days. Mixing takes place in a room designed for this purpose in my flat. If there are mixes to be done, you can set a time frame of one to two days per track, i.e. around 15 hours of concentrated listening. For a CD production with ten tracks, three weeks should definitely be planned.

Hamburg, July 18, 2017, Werner Kolb

On August 2, I received the message that the MD had decided to maintain my sick leave status. This did not change my assessment of the unspeakable nature of the whole process.

On the same day, I had my final session with Mr. Kroll. We agreed to meet again at the end of October to see how my tinnitus had developed.

»You have to expect it to get louder at first. Over the weeks, however, it will become quieter. The pressure in your ears will also slowly decrease. I recommend taking ›vitamin b‹ tablets for the next two months.«

I tried different preparations. Due to the constant fluctuations during this period, it was difficult to evaluate. But I am sure that taking it caused sleep disturbances in the form of nightmares and a louder noise in my ears. There is no doubt that both got better after I stopped taking it.

It rained a lot in August and I got pressure in both ears that lasted for three days. Perhaps the high humidity and the associated air pressure were responsible for this. I also had the impression that the valerian was having less and less effect. I could tell from the sensation in my legs, which was no longer present in the way I had known it from the first few months.

I had hardly dealt with my distortion for a long time. Of all the discomforts, it had moved into the background. When it did come to mind, it seemed to have diminished. My tinnitus decreased and approached the level of the end of April – slowly but steadily.

Now, after almost eight months, I entered the phase where I did very little. I went to my weekly psychother-apy sessions and, when the time was right, to yoga at ›Sport Spaß‹. From time to time, I did technical exercises on the instrument so as not to lose contact completely.

I missed playing live less and less. I no longer felt like the masses of gigs, and certainly not the volume. Above all, I didn't have to go to events where some pissheads stagger onto the stage and shout something in your ear while you're playing. I enjoyed the freedom of being able to go to bed at ten o'clock on a Saturday night if I wanted to. From a certain point of view, burdens had fallen away from me.

The Caribbean

Some time ago, I saw a report on television that focused on everyday life in a monastery. I found the atmosphere in which the monks lived very oppressive. As far as I remember, their day started at five o'clock. The ritualized routine consisted of praying, working, studying and eating, with hardly any talking. Some of them explained that the key to not going crazy was a clear structure. Each of the activities had a fixed time and duration.

A big challenge for me was to organize the days in such a way that I gave myself and my ears the opportunity to rest and relax without just killing time. Now I don't want to compare my everyday life with that of these monks, but: without having planned it, my days were given a formal structure.

After getting up, I sat down at the computer, did office work and all kinds of organizational tasks. Anything related to my flat – cleaning, tidying up, shopping – was scheduled for early afternoon, and usually accompanied by a short walk around my neighbourhood. This was followed by an evening relaxation period: the time when I read, surfed the internet or watched TV quietly.

There was a street festival on Große Bergstraße. I spotted the stand of a chiropractic practice and decided to take the opportunity. After a few minutes of waiting, I was led to a separate area. Following an assistant's measurement of my body, I went into a horizontal position and Felix Obra started his examination. The results showed that some of my upper cervical vertebrae were clearly twisted. He was very friendly and invited me to an information evening, which was to take place in his practice a few days later. I was already feeling quite well again, and there was no urgent need. Curiosity made me go to the evening and listen attentively to his presentation. I wanted to give it a try.

During the first treatment, the cracking sound when the cervical vertebrae were adjusted was extremely loud and my body felt a lot fresher afterwards.

The tinnitus became worse for a day, coupled with the familiar sleep problems. But here, too, the rule applied: the main thing is that something happens, even if it gets worse at first.

I had Mr. Obra adjust me a total of four times. It was an interesting experience, but I didn't feel the need to come in more often. On the one hand, I felt well-supported with laser therapy, psychotherapy, and, if desired, acupuncture. Secondly, none of the treatments I had in connection with my bones had any noticeable effect on my tinnitus. And last but not least, this was also a measure that I had to pay for everything myself.

Throughout the months, I rarely had any visitors. Even friends and colleagues, who had always placed great value on their empathic abilities and knew how I was doing, hadn't tried to contact me once. However, I myself was still caught up in the idea that it wasn't me, the sick person, who had the ball in my court, but that the others should reach out to me. I now see this as a misjudgement, as it is not particularly helpful when trying to successfully combat the process of loneliness.

I've known Jürgen since 1997, when we played together in the orchestra of the musical ›Hair‹ at the Lübeck Theatre. He was the guitarist, I was the bass sub. Our contact never broke off, and over the years we played together again and again in projects. I would even go so far as to say that a friendship has developed from it, which survives even several-month breaks unscathed. Jürgen was one of the few who called me regularly, and so it happened that he invited Petra and me to a concert: Stadtpark Open Air LOTTO KING KARL & DIE BARMBEK DREAM BOYS on September 23, 2017.

»Hey Werner, I'm playing as a sub for Lotto again. It takes place outdoors, and the maximum level must not exceed 90dB due to official regulations.«

»All right, we'd love to come.«

On the way through the city park, we passed the meadow that had been the venue for the ROLLING-STONES-concert two weeks earlier. Dude, it looked like that! Ploughed field was the more appropriate term.

Finally, we reached the area in front of the open-air stage. The support act was already playing and I hesitated. What am I going to do when everything is at full blast again afterwards? Petra looked at me. »Should we go again?«

»No, I want to go through with it now.« We passed the security check and entered the concert site. Earplugs and earmuffs came into action after a few minutes. The feeling in my body reminded me of the IRON-MAIDEN-concert, albeit toned down. After the break, we listened to another twenty minutes of Lotto and then left. For now, that was enough.

Three days later, I got another clear reaction from my body. The tinnitus swelled again, but did not reach the level of the first relapse.

By now, I was aware that I would have to expect and cope with such level fluctuations in intensity. In the long term, the tinnitus would disappear, or at least decrease to a level where I no longer notice it prominently, of that I was sure. Even a sleepless night no longer worried me. I had experienced too many of those in the last few months and knew that it would soon change again.

***

The CASH BOYS had become a firm institution on Hans-Albers-Platz and were active in one of the clubs every weekend. They were usually packed, there was a lot of alcohol being consumed, and visibility was obscured by cigarette smoke. The music from the DJ systems' loudspeakers was really loud. You couldn't necessarily call it nice, but it got everyone in the mood. In terms of rock, we were one of the most authentic bands and definitely one of the loudest here.

The stages were close to the audience, and you could literally smell each other's sweat. That was an advantage to get the proverbial sparks across, but it could also be extremely annoying.

Offel once got into a fight in the ›Drafthouse‹ with a guy who was built like a brick shithouse and was constantly provocative. I have no idea what it was about. At some point it got too much for Offel. He walked off the stage with his guitar and knocked this idiot out with a single, well-aimed punch. A classic knockout, Mike Tyson sent his regards. There was a scuffle with a few of the knocked-out man's buddies until bouncers defused the situation.

The music consisted only of bass and drums temporarily during the boxing match. Eventually, Offel came back on stage, slightly damaged from a headbutt.

At the end of the night, we received the news that the whole gang was waiting at Hans-Albers-Platz to intercept him. That morning, we collectively disappeared through the back exit.

One evening, when I wanted to go back into ›Molly Malone‹ after a break outside, the bouncer blocked my way.

»You stay outside.«

»You're funny, I'm part of the band.«

After the gig, I approached him.

»Tell me, why didn't you let me in?«

»Dude, you had an extremely aggressive vibe. If I let people like you in, trouble is guaranteed.«

His comment got me thinking and a little later I decided to quit the scene and the CASH BOYS. I think the bouncers here do a great job.

***

I was torn for several reasons when Offel asked me in October 2017 if I could help out for two gigs.

»We're playing at the ›Zwick‹ on Millerntorplatz. It'll be really quiet, I will only play the acoustic guitar.«

I knew for sure that it would definitely be loud, in the truest sense of the word. But it was too tempting, pure nostalgia. And it was really fun again, despite all the tension.

»I'm going crazy, as soon as Werner stands there, the people go wild.« These words from the mouth of a loyal fan from the old days were a blessing to my soul.

It went as expected and got pretty loud, both around me and inside me. To my astonishment, however, I realized that after a week it was back to the level it was at before the gigs.

A few weeks later, in November, a cruise was on my schedule that I had been hired for in the summer of 2016. It was supposed to be the first one that I wouldn't be doing with Klaus, but with DENNIS DURANT, a well-known soul singer from Hamburg. The two-week trip would take us through the Caribbean.

Despite all my reservations, I decided not to cancel. I hoped that the trip would give me a feeling for the extent to which I could even consider a permanent return to my job. There was a lot to deal with: the stress of a nine-hour flight, the constant background noise of a cruise ship, the concerts and the associated rehearsals.

»Mr. Kolb, this is a good opportunity. But I have to end your sick leave for that. If it doesn't work out, I'll write you a sick note again. If it's the same diagnosis, you'll go back on sick pay immediately.« Dr. Pielke's statement was confirmed by my health insurance company.

He also discussed the possibility of a psychosomatic rehab with me. However, I couldn't come to terms with the fact that I would be completely absent for six weeks. Angela, my neighbour, always looked after Elli in my absence. But two weeks was the maximum I wanted to put them both through. The idea of a day clinic, on the other hand, became more and more appealing to me. I dug out the brochure that had been lying in a file marked *Miscellaneous* for many months and made an appointment with Dr. Friedhelm Schreiber, the senior physician. I arrived at his office three days before the start of my sea voyage. He made a reserved impression as he took up his interview position with his legs crossed.

»What do you expect from a stay with us? Your tinnitus is significantly better, and you are already undergoing outpatient psychotherapy?«

That was a good question, especially since I was not yet clear on the details of what this clinic had to offer.

»There are two pillars: One consists of individual and group psychotherapeutic sessions. The other includes various forms of relaxation techniques such as meditation and Feldenkrais. The stay with us is usually six weeks, Monday to Friday from eight to three thirty. It is best to complete your cruise first and see how you are doing. Then we'll sit down together again.«

I left the clinic with a positive impression and decided to contact Mr. Kroll again before my trip.

»Sometimes it also gets louder when I'm travelling by car or train for a long time.«

»It often happens that the tinnitus gets louder when travelling by car. How long did it always last?«

»It was back to its old level after about a week, both after the concerts and the trips.«

»That's great. That means your ears are already so strong again that they can regenerate on their own, even if it takes several days. However, you should still be careful and continue to wear your ear protection. Let's meet again after your cruise.«

***

The contact with Dennis, a frontman representative who knows how to skilfully use his charm, came about a few years earlier through one of my fire brigade assignments. With Alex, a keyboard player, I had been playing regularly at the Große Freiheit in St. Pauli for some time.

I was out with Petra when the phone rang. Alex asked if I had time and desire to play with Dennis at a hotel on the Baltic Sea the next day. Although our weekend plans were different, after a brief consultation, I agreed.

A few weeks later, Dennis asked me to join a tour. A hotel chain had hired an agency to book him. The management's idea behind this was to give their hotel chain's old-fashioned image a breath of fresh air. To this end, various branches throughout Germany are planned to be played over a period of two weeks. However, the advertising seemed makeshift from the start. An ad was placed on the hotel's website and posters were hung on site bulletin boards stating that tickets could be purchased in advance or at the door – that's it.

We rehearsed our program and finally the production, which consisted of seven musicians and two technicians including sound and lighting equipment, was set to start. Then, the agency informed us that, contrary to expectations, advance sales had been a little slow. One of the branches wanted to cancel the date without substitution, which was done after a small exchange of opinions in return for a corresponding expense allowance.

The tour kick-off took place in Hamburg. The hotel looked classy, the stage area was spacious and the hall was well-filled. Everyone involved was in a great mood and the audience was enthusiastic. We said goodbye with the certainty of having a great tour ahead of us.

It quickly became clear that our first venue was the most modern building in the chain. The others were noticeably older and looked very dusty. Soon the suspicion arose that the impetus from this soul tour might be a little weak to set a change in motion. The longer it went on, the more manageable the number of visitors became. Soon there was no longer a box office, or it was packed away after a very short time. Meanwhile, every guest who wandered into the concert hall to relax after an exhausting day was appreciated. Anyone who bought a ticket in advance was simply out of luck. The agency did not communicate with us anymore. A good example of how exposed you are as a band when someone doesn't do their job.

In these moments, Dennis also showed what it means to be professional and a good band leader. We didn't let our spirits get dampened and enjoyed our colleagues' solo interludes. After our work was done, we hung out in the lobby or collectively nested in one of our rooms to reduce the contents of the minibars. The everyday life of a musician.

***

As a preparatory measure for the cruise, I had started listening to music at a low volume of seventy dB every day. I used an app to monitor this. As soon as my ears responded, which happened after about twenty minutes in the form of a slight pressure, I ended the experiment.

On the day of departure, the band met at the airport at three o'clock in the afternoon. Everyone was aware of my situation, and I would like to thank Dennis and my colleagues for their exceptional thoughtfulness. My tinnitus, which had calmed down more and more in the past few weeks, consisted of a slight hissing noise, comparable to the sound of water running through pipes in the wall.

The travel plan initially involved a one-hour flight to London. There we spent the night in a hotel on the airport grounds before flying on to the Bahamas in the early morning. Even during this first flight, the water pipe turned into a canoe trip to Niagara Falls.

For a long time, a major problem had been environments with different sources of noise, such as those found in restaurants or pubs: people talking, the clattering of dishes, along with piped music. These situations were unbearable with or without earplugs; it was completely impossible to hold a conversation.

After checking in, we met in the hotel restaurant. There was quite a lot of noise here, and the hiss in my head got even more animated. After a drink, I felt stressed and prepared myself for an expected increase in noise during the long-haul flight.

Having completed an early morning odyssey with checking out of the hotel, transferring to the airport, checking in luggage, going through security and boarding, we took off as planned. I started reading a book. After about three hours, my tinnitus increased significantly, but I managed to block it out. Another two hours later, it ramped up even more and reached a level that reminded me of my first Trental phase. After landing, there was a half-hour bus ride to the ship. Here we went into the reception hall, a large, open space. This meant that it did not absorb the sound, but rather amplified it. Several hundred passengers, most of them new arrivals like us, were chatting. Champagne was served, a pianist played the grand piano, and check-in took place at the same time. The noise in my head was at its peak. I kept taking deep breaths and longed for the moment when it would be quiet around me.

It took a good hour before I was sitting on the sofa in my cabin. Soberly, I calculated how long this state would last. First, two weeks on the ship with rehearsals and concerts, then the return flight with its expectedly similar effects. Then a good two weeks to subside again.

Our first concert took place four days after setting sail, which was good. This at least gave my ears a chance to calm down a bit. The noise from the ship was surprisingly low and I didn't feel like it was bothering me. The rehearsal was relaxed, and the concert that evening was a great success.

When I got to my cabin, my ears were ringing violently. Nevertheless, I was still able to sleep well, which remained the case throughout the entire journey. To my surprise, everything had calmed down the next morning, and it even seemed quieter than before the concert.

The further development turned out to be surprisingly positive. Within a good week, the tinnitus had become much quieter. After the rehearsals and concerts, it always swelled up, but only for a day. By the end of the cruise, it had decreased to a much lower level compared to how I felt when arriving at the reception hall. During the nine-hour flight from Miami to Frankfurt, I only experienced a slight increase.

Of course, I thought that was great, but I couldn't put my finger on it. On the outward flight, I had suspected that it could be due to the pressure differences caused by the cruising altitude of more than eleven kilometres. Now my suspicion was more in the direction of stress, which was lower on the return flight.

Although not with the result I had hoped for, this trip had clearly shown me how I should proceed. I would go back on sick leave, avoid any kind of loud noise and stress in the coming weeks, and go to the day clinic as soon as possible.

I had already discussed with Petra weeks ago that we wouldn't participate in any family celebrations for Christmas or travel to southern Germany. For the days around New Year's Eve, we rented a cottage in the countryside to spend the holidays in peace.

A good plan.

The Day Clinic

For months now, I've been haunted by minor hearing loss. At least that's what I call them. Similar to when you flick a light switch and it suddenly goes dark, there was a pop in one of my ears, and I was completely deaf on that one. The noise was also gone. A few seconds later, a sound faded in – the ›Enterprise‹ came from the depths of starless space and flew past my imaginary eyes until it disappeared from view again. Then the light was slowly turned up by a dimmer.

This process, from the fade-in to the slow disappearance of the sound and the return of hearing, lasted between ten and sixty seconds. Initially, this happened irregularly every few days, but now it occurs several times per hour. I then imagined that individual auditory nerves were being re-erected at these moments.

A few days after my return, I found myself once again at Dr. Pielke's office. I wanted to get sick pay as soon as possible. While I was waiting, I read one of the rare interviews with Sebastian Deisler in a magazine: the exceptional talent of German football, who decided to end his career at a young age due to a long series of injuries and depression. Among other things, he described how anxiety was always a factor for him in the end. Hopefully, the cruciate ligament will remain intact. With every sprint, every duel. This made it impossible for him to concentrate on the game as necessary to perform at the required level and to find joy in it.

I've never read or heard anything that described my situation more accurately. Fear was a constant companion at every one of my gigs over the last few months, and the

›I hope everything goes well‹ was ever-present. I could no longer let myself fall into the music. The joy was gone. It had long been clear that – faced with the choice between making music and calm in my head – I would choose the second.

***

At the beginning of 2015, I performed with a band in a small club. Our program consisted of quiet, partly melancholic original compositions. There was a homeless man sitting at the front door opposite the bar, who seemed to be here often and took the opportunity to warm up. From the very first song, he drew attention to himself by commenting loudly on what was happening on and in front of the stage. I observed how individual guests soon started talking at him, but this had no noticeable effect. The guy was incredibly annoying, quite apart from the disrespect shown here.

After the break, things continued in the same way and my adrenaline was pumping more and more. Suddenly, we heard him shouting: »I have to go on stage and congratulate the guitarist on his solo.«

No sooner said than done! The asshole set off, stomping loudly. That was the signal that it was time to intervene. This dude wasn't going to set foot on the stage.

I put the bass in the stand, walked up to the guy and clearly indicated with an outstretched hand that it was the end of the line. He didn't want to be deterred. I had to be more forceful, raised the volume of my voice, ripped the cap off his head and threw it into a corner. Next, a guest came to protect him from me. To some, it looked as if I had slapped him in the face. Then, after he was escorted to safety with a ›But I just wanted to congratulate the guitarist‹ stammer, another guest intervened.

»The bass player should apologize.«

This demand was met with overwhelming agreement. A discussion ensued in which I argued that I was not the one who needed to apologize. But it was clear to the public who was the asshole here. To smooth things over, I went outside to have a chat with the lovely gentleman. When he also demanded a public apology, I asked him if he was otherwise healthy, and whispered a few charming things in his ear, that I won't repeat here. I went back into the club, and he followed a little later.

»Is everything settled?« The question was directed exclusively at my opponent.

»We're one hundred percent smooth.« Well then.

The concert could go on, the mood was of course subdued. We played three more songs, received a lukewarm applause, and began to dismantle our equipment. It was remarkable that the guest in question didn't make a single sound after he had taken his seat again.

Once I finished loading my car, I had a chat with the club owner, who was standing behind the bar, and one of the guests, who had loudly demanded my apology.

»A society has to put up with someone like that.« So there, aha. For both of them, I was still the bad guy in the story. The interesting part was the identical conclusion they independently formulated: »Oh, you know, at least he was quiet afterwards.«

Check it out! I went home feeling like I was officially the bad guy of the night, but some attendees were secretly pretty happy that someone had put him in his place.

***

Dr. Pielke issued me with a sick note and a referral slip for the day clinic. A few days later, I was going to it, sitting with Dr. Schreiber.

»Well then, tell me about it. How did you fare during the journey?«

»Unfortunately, not as I had hoped.«

He listened carefully to what I had to say.

»I can well imagine that a stay with us will help you. We will also give you the tools you need to deal better with such stressful situations in the future.«

I went into the office to complete the formalities. It was a strange feeling as I filled out the registration form.

»How long do you think the waiting time will be?«

»I can't tell you exactly, but for tinnitus patients it's usually only a couple of weeks.«

Over the next few days, my thoughts turned to what was to come. But although I woke up several times a night, I was able to sleep well. After two weeks, the phone rang.

»Mr. Kolb, we can offer you January 4, 2018 as a possible start date for therapy.«

Without hesitation, I agreed. The Christmas holidays went as planned and New Year's Eve passed without a hitch.

My first day was limited to a brief introduction. I was shown around the premises and the procedures were explained to me. There was a kind of timetable like the one I knew from school, which was displayed on a blackboard. I was surprised, as there were only few program points with longer breaks in between. I had expected to find completely structured days. After all, I had to sign that nothing that happened here would leak out.

I arrived at eight o'clock on the dot the next morning. The days always began with a welcome round, where each group member described how they had started the day and how they were feeling. This meeting lasted fifteen minutes and I introduced myself. Then we went to our common area and had our first get-to-know-you conversations. The arrival was made easy for me, I felt immediately welcomed.

Each group had different focuses. Mine was called ›Tinnitus and Stress‹, where stress stood for depression, which was very pronounced in some. The size of it changed during the weeks. With people coming and going, vacant spots were not immediately filled. However, the number of participants was always in single figures and half of them were fellow sufferers, although not professional colleagues.

I was still a passive listener and observer. Some impressions of the first few days really shook me up, and I got slightly misty-eyed when I sat on the bus on the way home, reviewing what I had heard.

I would describe the company atmosphere as relaxed. Attendance was compulsory for the program points, but in the phases in between we could leave the premises at any time and take care of other things. I was still very careful and wore my ear protection for the bus rides. I also used it from time to time during breaks because it was sometimes very loud in the public areas. I didn't go to lunch, which was taken in nearby restaurants. The effects of the cruise had too much of a grip on me.

In the group sessions, I often thought how happy I was to be mentally well again. A year ago, I would have been sitting here quite differently. It got very emotional at times, and I was confronted with all kinds of emotions, including negative ones. Sometimes the scenery reminded me of a backstage room where you retreat to as a band during breaks. It wasn't always peace, joy, and happiness there either.

I noticed the anxiety of some companions as they realized that their time here was coming to an end. My therapy with Dr. Herzfeld was just postponed. I could seamlessly go back to her afterwards – a good feeling.

There was an incident in the fourth week. When I asked why I hadn't yet received any notification of sick pay, I was initially confronted with a call from my health insurance company: »Mr. Kolb, you can only start receiving sick pay from the seventh week onwards. This is otherwise not possible for freelancers under the Artists' Social Security Act.«*

A staff member of the Independent Patient Advisory Service Germany (UPD) confirmed this to me: »You can, of course, try to take legal action against this on the basis of the guaranteed prompt payment. In my opinion, however, there is little chance of success.«

I had received incorrect information beforehand. It's pretty crazy that even health insurance employees don't know exactly how their system works. Shortly after, I was informed in writing about the amount of the new sickness benefit and found that it had been revised downwards.

»As this is a new sick note and your income from the last twelve months is used as the basis for calculation, it is lower than before.«

That's right, I was on sick leave at the time. It was now seventy percent of seventy percent, but for some reason I didn't care. I didn't assume any malice from any of the parties involved. For me, it was just another lesson in bureaucratic procedures. In fact, all information should be checked personally, even if it comes from the relevant authorities themselves.

But who does that?

But now to the essentials. There were program items that took place independently of the group. One of these was a choir with an alternative to meditation. The respective group therapist decided which event each person would be assigned to. With this in mind, I was always relieved that psychologist Anton Friesinger put my name down for meditation. This time my heart missed a beat, I saw myself in the choir.

---

* See ›Notes‹ at the end of the book (Page 144): **Letter of the Health Insurance Company**

At my first appointment with Dr. Schreiber, we had passed a room from which incredibly loud, unstructured drumming and hysterical singing had emanated. Reflexively I flinched. It was the choir.

I can't remember how many times I left and came back to check if there was still ›choir‹, and started to tremble. I had spoken more than once about my greatest fear: that my tinnitus could become loud again because of noise and at some point not go away again. Hadn't anyone listened to me? I ran into the office.

»Is there a mistake here? It must be an oversight by Mr. Friesinger.«

»If that's how it's entered, it will be correct. He has certainly thought it through.«

I boycotted the event and spent the rest of the day huddled up in the relaxation room. I felt completely helpless, as if someone wanted to deliberately lead me into a trap.

During the evening farewell round, I collapsed, could hardly say a sentence, rejected all the therapist's offers and left the premises in a hurry.

It was Friday. I spent most of the weekend lying on the sofa, kept getting cramps and decided to stop the therapy.

On Monday morning, I called the clinic to let them know. That same evening, my phone rang and the clinic's doctor, Dr. Katja Sellmer, was on the line.

»You weren't here today. What's wrong with you?«

She was unaware of the incident. Her warm-hearted manner led to a pleasant conversation. But I was not dissuaded from my decision.

It was a confusing night, during which I realized that I had been fooling myself regarding my mental state. I hadn't fallen into a comparable hole in a long time. As the night progressed, I understood that terminating the therapy would be a big mistake.

Not to run away, but to face the challenge. That was the point. I was still of the opinion that things had gone badly. But I increasingly saw the opportunity I had here and that I shouldn't throw it away lightly. The phone call with Dr. Sellmer had a significant influence on this development.

I got up at six o'clock with the intention of reversing the abortion, and was able to intercept Dr. Schreiber on his arrival before the start of the day's program.

»I'm pleased about your change of heart. As we always wait a little while until the discharge papers are ready, nothing has happened yet. You can continue your therapy without any problems.«

I was first asked to see Mr. Friesinger, who wanted to explain his decision to me using an example: »If someone is afraid to stand in line at a supermarket checkout, the approach is to repeatedly confront the person with the situation. The aim is to gradually reduce the fear.«

I tried to explain to him what the crucial difference was. At no point was it about reducing any kind of phobia or fear in me, but about preventing a physical relapse with possible long-term consequences. »Even if the comparison is a bit of a stretch, to stick with your example, you have to consider the possibility of the person ending up in a wheelchair for the rest of their life because they've been in a queue for so long.«

I didn't get the impression that he understood or wanted to understand. In my opinion, he told me that he had no idea what tinnitus meant and what the consequences of such noise exposure could be.

After that night, the phrase ›I need to sleep on it‹ took on a completely new meaning for me.

I never went to choir.

***

For me, I have long made a distinction between bands that perform concerts – and those that offer services. Concerts take place in front of an audience that listens and usually last ninety minutes. Services include dance events of all kinds. The music mainly consists of covers and the playing times extend over several hours. It doesn't matter whether *Please Release Me* or *Highway to Hell* is presented. Playing with a service band on New Year's Eve is normally a good thing. An unwritten rule states that double the fee is paid on this day. From a financial point of view, it is a very lucrative, if not the best day of the year. This makes the jobs that are available here all the more coveted. I earned by far the most at the millennium. The manager of my band at the time negotiated a fee that exceeded the typical monthly salary.

In the first decade of the new millennium, my path led me to a funk & soul band, which meant that primarily American sound of these styles was played. Of course, there were songs that were well-known from the charts. However, the topicality and flexibility of the program could not be compared with that of a dance band or Top-40 band. That's why the opportunities to perform were rather limited. And when the news came that we had a New Year's Eve gig in a prestigious hotel in the south of Hamburg, it was a very good thing for all of us, because it wasn't a matter of course.

On December 30, the band met for a rehearsal. The cell phone of our singer, who was the contact person for the organizers, rang. A representative of our management was on the line: we would be playing this gig as a replacement for another band and would therefore not be performing under our band name, but under theirs.

When he told us this, it was immediately clear that this was not kosher. My first thought was not to approve it under any circumstances, and in hindsight that would have been the only sensible reaction to such a rally.

We talked about it in the band, and the possibility of cancelling the gig was discussed, but not decided. Such a reaction would also cause problems. It wasn't just that the fee we thought we had already in our hands would suddenly disappear. Someone had signed contracts that normally contain a clause entitled ›contractual penalty‹. This means that the band could be held accountable if they cancel without a valid reason or force majeure. The fact that we only received this message the day before the big event severely limited our ability to react.

So we drove to the prestigious venue, put on our suits, and began to entertain the illustrious guests with our melodies. They were unmistakably in a pay grade that was well above average.

It quickly became clear that what was coming out of the speakers wasn't what our customers had expected and hoped for. The dance floor remained demonstratively empty and the displeasure in the hall was clearly noticeable. It so happened that the hotel manager appeared in our dressing room during the first long break. Slowly, he closed the door behind him and uttered a sentence that was almost unbelievably absurd:

»Tell me, who are you actually?«

This was followed by our singer's awkward attempt to explain. It was an extremely unpleasant situation for both parties.

»The fee will not be paid until this has been clarified with those responsible.«

We held an emergency sitting to decide whether we should continue playing at all. There were representatives for both options. Due to a majority decision, we chose to fulfil the contract and played until three in the morning.

We were very sorry for the guests, and not least for the hotel manager. Some had paid a lot of money for an unforgettable New Year's Eve – which, seen the other way round, had been delivered to them. The manager had to take responsibility and faced the prospect of receiving fewer bookings for the upcoming year.

When we asked our agent how this could have happened, we were met with absolute incomprehension.

»The other band's management had received a demo from you and knew what kind of music you're playing.« In the end, the situation was never clarified, let alone a fee paid.

The whole thing became a running joke. Whenever I met a colleague from that night on other occasions, the phrase »Tell me, who are you actually?« was repeated.

In the end, this New Year's Eve became an experience that everyone involved could tell their proverbial grandchildren about.

***

After my stay in the day clinic, I was given the opportunity of an office job. One of those jobs where you just sit in front of a computer screen, which was perfect for me. It had nothing to do with loudness and was actually fun. The most important thing was that I could finally end my sick leave status, which, when looking at it soberly, had caused me a lot of stress, without having to finance my rent through music.

I thought about whether I was not entirely innocent of the relapses. Had I perhaps closed my ears off too much?

I devised a step-by-step strategy to get used to loudness again: leaving the construction site earmuffs off when washing up and vacuuming was one of them. Putting them on had become such a routine that I first had to get used to not doing it automatically.

On the occasion of our anniversary, I invited Petra to a theatre performance. A few days later, after many years, I went back as a guest to ›Birdland‹, the jazz club where I used to play so much in my early days in Hamburg. All without ear protection. I observed and noticed that the level in my head only increased for a short time, if at all. So far, so good. But what about making music now?

Over the past fifteen months, I have endured fears like never before in my life: That the tinnitus would stay as loud as it is. That it would get louder.

I missed the fact that I could no longer sit at my favourite listening place, enjoy the subtleties of a good production, go on a journey. But playing live? Petra had often asked me if I missed that as well. The answer was always the same: not really.

A phase began in which I realized that I was in a situation I had never imagined – and a positive one at that. I was able to set a new course. Everything back to square one. Thanks to tinnitus.

Why did I actually systematically hide myself under the influence for several decades from the age of fourteen? Why did I actually start making music? Why did I actually go to Hamburg back then? When did it actually all start heading in a direction that wasn't fun anymore and why the hell didn't I react? Who was I actually?

If I continue to make music, it won't be rock anymore. Quieter, more relaxed realms. Experience has taught me that the question ›do you also play double bass?‹ is unavoidable. Why not?

So I decided to get a new instrument for my new beginning. I developed an in-ear concept that allowed me to protect my ears and have good control over myself.

I started jamming irregularly with colleagues at room volume. Sometimes I got the feeling of a slight inflammation in my right ear, which was gone the next day.

My tinnitus slowly, but steadily, became quieter with the familiar fluctuations. A stock curve that moved in the

typical zigzag towards zero, which in this case repre-
sented the optimal course. Whether this was due to the
time factor, rest, one of the therapies, or all together, I
could not judge, nor did I care.

It wasn't long before a good opportunity arose for me to
immerse myself in the music scene again. I had played
with Judith Tellado in Dennis Durant's band on the Caribbean cruise. She was looking for a double bass player for
her band, and I became a permanent member.

Months later, when I was sitting in the dressing room
after one of our concerts with Judith, Georg (piano) and
Paulo (saxophone), I realized, that I hadn't thought about
my tinnitus during the whole performance, that I wasn't
afraid of a relapse. The first time in two years.

What was that feeling like? At first, of course, great.
But I noticed that it no longer had the same significance
for me. There are so many options for activities that have
nothing to do with loudness or music.

Why not do something completely different.

Why not write a book.

Piet

In November 2013, around the same time as I started my training as a sound engineer, I adopted two cats from the animal shelter. Originally, I wanted a dog, but since I was frequently travelling at that time and wouldn't have been able to bring a dog along, I decided on cats instead. I got the go-ahead from my landlord and started looking for animals that were used to living indoors and didn't know how to go outside. I wanted two so they wouldn't be alone during my absence. Preferably striped and not too young.

I drove by car to Süderstraße and let myself be guided through the rooms of the shelter. When we entered the third room, two animals that were together in one of the cages immediately came to the bars. They were the first to show such curiosity. The larger of the two had a black and white coat, the smaller a completely black one. At first the black and white was in front, then the other one pushed forwards and took command. It was clear that she was the more dominant one. It should be these two.

I prepared my flat for the impending addition. I installed a balcony net, a scratching post, climbing facilities, litter boxes and everything else that was needed.

Armed with two transport boxes, I set off a few days later to pick them up. The handover was unspectacular. A member of staff took them out of the cage, put them in my carriers, and I could leave. They cried a little on the way to the car and during the drive.

When I opened the boxes in my flat, they immediately came out and started to explore their new surroundings. The litter box was identified as such and inaugurated after just a few minutes, which I took note of very favourably. It was only then that I realized they weren't striped, but there's always something.

I named the black and white Elli and the tomcat Piet. They settled in quickly and made use of everything I had prepared for them. I noticed that Piet's fur was much duller than Elli's.

It turned out that Elli was not a lap cat. But she liked to be near me and preferred to lie down on the nearest table to get her scratching sessions: desk, kitchen table, living room table. She became my table cat.

With Piet, it took a few days before he signalled for the first time that he wanted to sit on my lap. After that, there were fixed times for this. Sometimes, when I had made myself comfortable on the sofa, he would lie on my tummy, neck, or face.

In the evenings, they would have their wrestling matches and chase each other around the flat, including damaging some wallpaper, which didn't bother me. Piet was a real bully, Elli was rather calmer. Mostly, she withdrew when they got into a fight, even though she was far superior to him physically.

Together with the automatic feeders, everything worked really well. If I was away for more than twenty-four hours, Angela, my neighbour, took care of them. Time passed and Elli and Piet became more and more a part of my life.

During a car ride through Hamburg, I happened to see an advertisement on a house façade saying: ›Veterinarian comes to your house‹. I thought this was great, as it spared both myself and the animals the stress of going to a clinic.

I wanted to try this out to have them vaccinated. During the examination with the stethoscope, it turned out that Elli didn't like it at all, whereas Piet had no problem with it. He also kept completely still during the vaccination, while Elli screamed terribly and could hardly be restrained. In the end, everything was over, and I decided that I only wanted to put her through that in future if it was really necessary.

After about two years, Piet stopped eating from one day to the next. It wasn't unusual for them not to eat so well. However, I immediately had concerns and contacted the vet. She came the next day, examined him and found that his kidneys were very large. I put Piet back in a carrier for the first time since I got him and drove to a veterinary clinic in the north of Hamburg. During the drive, he cried again as he had done back then, and I also shed a few tears. I drove with the feeling that these would be our last moments together.

At the clinic, he was examined again. The doctor's first reaction was pessimistic, and I had already resigned myself to the impending euthanasia. Then she suggested that a biopsy could be done, and they could try to boost him with infusions. Piet put up with everything and looked at me with his faithful eyes while I was scratching him.

Four days later, Petra and I picked him up from the clinic. Something happened in my flat that I hadn't expected at all. Elli sniffed at him and started hissing wildly, rejecting him completely. I felt sorry for Piet, as he was visibly weakened. He crawled under the bed in the bedroom and was rarely seen. Every time he crossed Elli's path, she became aggressive, and I was afraid that things could get worse.

After a few days, the phone rang. The examination of the biopsy revealed that it was a malignant tumour. They mentioned considering chemotherapy, which I immediately declined. I thought that a week ago, I should have followed my instincts and spared Piet these days. I asked the vet to come and put him to sleep.

When she arrived the next day, Piet was lying under my bed. I got him out, took him to the living room table, and placed him on a towel I had spread out beforehand. The first injection was still in him when he slumped to the side and came to lie on it. While the vet listened to him repeatedly with the stethoscope and finally administered the second, final injection, I cuddled him. I had the impression that he passed gently.

One of my first sessions with Dr. Herzfeld was about how I could deal with situations in which I wasn't feeling well.

»You can try to remember events that made you feel comfortable.«

I remembered that as a child I was always happy when I was with my grandparents.

During the last cruise, when I was sitting in my cabin in the evening with this incredible noise level in my head, I often thought of Elli. I imagined myself rubbing her belly as she lay on my desk in front of me. That really helped.

When I think back to that evening on December 30, 2016. I was sitting in the living room, reading the book that Petra had given me a few days earlier, and consciously enjoying this peace and quiet for the last time. Then I can hear it again, that incomparable sound of silence.

When I think of Piet, I can cry.

Epilogue

Why a book about tinnitus? There are already plenty of them out there. But is this really a book about tinnitus? Of course, but not only.

Without a concrete plan, I began creating a timeline of events and gradually fleshing it out. I had plenty of time for that. It was only later that stories from my life were added. On the one hand, they were intended to loosen things up, on the other hand, to provide approaches to the question that knows no answer: Why did it happen the way it did? I had a vision in mind right from the start. There was a barrel overflowing that had slowly filled up over a period of fifty years.

I would like to emphasize that this is not about condemning people or our healthcare system. I am describing the actual state of affairs as I experienced it, in the context of a symptom about whose origin little is known.

Some names and genders of the doctors, therapists, musicians, and friends have been changed. The events have all taken place as described. This does not mean that the statements made are necessarily correct. Similarly, my personal thoughts and associated conclusions do not claim to be universally valid. For example, it may not be uncommon for peace to return to the mind after adjusting the upper cervical vertebrae.

I am not of the opinion that tinnitus is a typical musician's disease. During my research, I came across the figure that ten percent of the German population suffer to a greater or lesser extent from ringing in the ears. That would be around eight million, and in my experience, the actual number is likely higher in such statistics. Of the many sufferers I have come across in the past seven years, only a few were professional colleagues. In the day clinic, I was the only one. Whether it's gradual, like mine, or triggered by a blast trauma, it can affect anyone. And if this book can do a little to inspire, encourage or take the pressure off, then it will have been worth all the effort. I wish I had got my hands on something like this at the beginning of my odyssey.

2017 was a dark year. The darkest I've experienced so far. The stories end in spring 2019. It was the year in which I could see light on the horizon again.

I got in touch with FRIEDERIKE LINSMEIER, a young singer, pianist and songwriter from Hamburg. We played several concerts together, most of them as a duo. Her positive attitude encouraged me to intensify my playing on the double bass and to look for a coach.

»I know someone, GIORGI KIKNADZE.«

Going back to school in my old age? – why not. More than thirty years after Detlev, Giorgi became my second teacher, an equally extraordinary musician and person.

The psychotherapy came to an end. All that remained of the medical treatments was laser therapy, which I still undergo at irregular intervals to this day.

Then came Covid. As my personal lockdown had already lasted three years, the developments in spring 2020 only affected me marginally. Initially, this was just the beginning of another period of time that I could use to give myself and my ears the rest they needed.

2023 was an exciting year. Among other things, I had to make a decision: Do I want to try to get back into the live business professionally, or do I call it a day for good.

To find out, I called Sven. A colleague I've known since the nineties and bass player in the ›Zwick house band‹.

»Hey Sven, I wanted to ask if it would be possible for me to drop by and play 2 or 3 songs. I want to get a feel for whether my ears can take it again.«

»Sure, no problem. Just come around on Saturday. We start at 10:30 pm.«

Right on time for the first set, Petra and I ordered our first beer and listened to the band. Dude, what noise level, what an endurance test. Then it was time. I was called on stage. I put in my 25dB earplugs, set on my woolly hat, strapped on the bass and off we went. Yes, there it was again – the fire, the energy, the passion, the joy.

»If you want, you can do the sub for me here from now on.« I wanted to and have played there a lot of gigs since then, becoming more and more confident. Fear had long since ceased to play a role.

At the turn of the year, I decided to use 2024 to regain a permanent place in the Hamburg music scene. And as if someone had been waiting for it, the news that would completely turn my life upside down reached me in mid-January – once again.

I had known Günter since 1988, an excellent guitarist with an impressive CV. He was one of the few who had known about my ear problems from the very beginning and had followed my journey from afar. But with the exception of a few sessions, we had never played together before.

»What about your ears now? Would you be interested and available to fill in as our bassist with VANJA SKY for 6 shows? We are touring throughout Europe all year, and there would surely be more requests for you.«

Wow, what an offer! My mind started to work. Was it perhaps still a bit too early? To cut a long story short, I accepted and prepared the 90-minute concert program, by heart of course.

One day before it was supposed to start, there was a rehearsal. The band was completed by Hannes, an established drummer in the Hamburg scene, with whom I had formed the rhythm section for projects several times over the decades.

My first concert with Vanja took place in Dortmund. I had the 12dB plugs in. The club was fully packed, and the place was buzzing from the first note.

What a band, what a lead singer.

And as life goes, a few weeks later Vanja called me.

»February 17th will be the last gig with my current bass player. Would you like to join permanently?«

Sometimes the light at the end of the tunnel really does come from a direction you wouldn't expect.

In September 2024, my tinnitus consists of a slight noise that I mostly do not perceive. The hyperacusis and the pressure in my ears are completely gone. The hearing distortion is still present to varying degrees. I do not rule out the possibility that it may also disappear again.

One last little anecdote at this point.

When it became clear that the studios would be allowed to reopen during the pandemic, I got really excited about getting a new tattoo. I had a few rough ideas; what was missing was real inspiration. A little unnerved, I finally browsed through a site with quotes from famous people. Then a shiver ran down my spine. Was this the root of all evil? I saw the little boy again, sitting in the back seat of his parents' car, looking out of the window and watching the stars. In search of a world in which he could be who he was.

»What's that supposed to mean?« Seba, my tattoo artist, frowned as we chose the font. Then he started his work. I closed my eyes. If only you knew what that means to me.

Power is being told
you are not loved
and not being destroyed by it
—

MADONNA

Acknowledgements

Last but not least, I would like to thank the people who have been with me in the last few years.

First and foremost Petra. You've been by my side since 2008. Sometimes I think I'm dreaming, because it's too good to be true. You caught me as I was falling.

To Gunnar Heyse, Jürgen Scholz, Nina Maleika, Steffen Dotter, Eva Deußing and Oliver Frei. Whether by email, Skype, phone or on my sofa, you were there.

To Ramon Kramer, Dennis Durant, Judith Tellado, Georg Sheljasov, Paulo Pereira, Micha Holland and Matthias Friedel, as well as Raimondo di Renzo, who engaged me for his ROYAL CHRISTMAS ORCHESTRA in December 2018. You gave me the opportunity to try my hand at music, regardless of the risks involved for you.

To Friederike Linsmeier and Giorgi Kiknadze, whom I probably would never have met without going through this disaster. What a stroke of luck and what a gift! You have accompanied me into my new musical phase of life.

To Volker ›Offel‹ Offelmann and Jan Polter for unforgettable years. Of all the things I've experienced, I would least like to miss our time together.

And finally to Vanja Sky, Günter Haas and Hannes Hoffmann. For seven years, I didn't know where my way would lead me. Now our paths have crossed.

I've been lucky once again.

Photo Credits

P. 3, 26, 83: Paintpictures / Pedi Wlosik
P. 11: Werner Kolb
P. 76, 117: Sven Arendt
P. 135: gudrun petersen / einzelbilder.com
P. 142: Petra Bendfeldt

Musiker & Tinnitus

On my YouTube channel
›Musiker&Tinnitus‹
I discuss all the topics
mentioned in this book in detail.
There is space for questions and discussion.

www.youtube.com / @wernerkolb

Letter of the Health Insurance Company

Dear Mr. Kolb

With reference to your email dated 11.01.2018, we would like to inform you of the following.

For those insured under the Artists' Social Insurance Act (KSVG), entitlement to sickness benefit arises at the beginning of the seventh week of incapacity for work (§46 Social Security Code V).

You have been unable to work since 04.12.2017, so the entitlement to sickness benefit would arise from 15.01.2018 in the event of continuous incapacity for work.

Section 3 of the Continued Remuneration Act (EFZG) generally regulates the entitlement to continued remuneration for groups of people who are in an employment relationship as employees.

As you are a self-employed artist and do not receive continued remuneration from an employer, we cannot consider the illness from 24.02.2017 to 06.11.2017 as a pre-existing illness.

Do you have any questions? Please give us a call.